Contents

How to use this book

Each page has a title telling you what it is about.

Instructions look like this. Always read these carefully before starting.

Read these word problems very carefully. Decide how you will work out the answers.

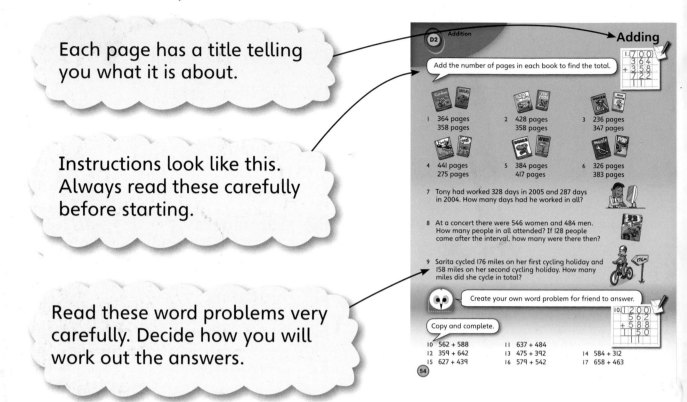

This shows you how to set out your work. The first question is done for you.

These are exploratory activities. You may want to discuss them with a partner.

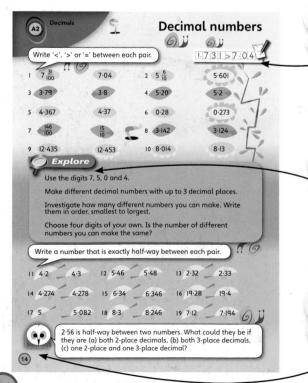

This is Owl. Ask your teacher if you need to do his questions.

Rounding

Write the position of each pointer, then round the number to the nearest:

1. a) 6 5 6 0 → 7 0 0 0

Round each price to the nearest (a) thousand pounds, (b) hundred pounds and (c) ten pounds.

4. a) £ 8 1 4 6 → £ 8 0 0 0
   b) £ 8 1 0 0
   c) ...

4 £8146
5 £7234
6 £3974
7 £9148
8 £5158
9 £11762
10 £12349
11 £6695
12 £15685

Write a 4-digit number which gives the same rounded number when rounded to the nearest thousand, hundred and ten.

3

Rounding

Round the number of words to the nearest (a) hundred and (b) ten. You can draw a number line to help.

1. 4 3 2 8 → a) 4 3 0 0 b) 4 3 3 0

1   Oliver Twiddle
    4328 words

2   Footy Facts
    6795 words

3   Dinosaur Planet
    3827 words

4   Classroom Mystery
    13 452 words

5   Fun at the Stables
    11 261 words

6   The School Legend
    8875 words

7   Tiger Escape
    6983 words

8   The Famous Seven
    8914 words

9   Sleep Walker
    9276 words

If Jayne reads these two books, find the total number of pages, then round it to the nearest hundred.

10 Oliver Twiddle
    and
    Fun at the Stables

11 Famous Seven
    and
    Dinosaur Planet

12 Sleep Walker
    and
    The School Legend

13 Footy Facts
    and
    Classroom Mystery

14 Tiger Escape
    and
    The School Legend

15 Oliver Twiddle
    and
    Sleep Walker

Explore

For each of questions 10–15, round both of the numbers to the nearest hundred, then add them.

Do you get same answer as if you added first, then rounded?

Rounding

These are the attendances at football matches. Round them to the nearest (a) thousand and (b) hundred.

1. 2 7 , 5 6 4   a) 2 8 , 0 0 0   b) 2 7 , 6 0 0

1 Rovers

27 564

2 City

18 546

3 Albion

43 582

4 United
13 712

5 Athletic
64 789

6 Wanderers
34 358

Find last Saturday's attendance figures at a football game. Round them to the nearest thousand and the nearest hundred.

7 At last Saturday's match there were 7652 adults and 2847 children. Find the total number of spectators. Round your answer to the nearest hundred. If each person bought a programme for £3, how much money was made?

£3

8  A club sold their striker for a fee of £51 465 and paid £37 374 for a new goalkeeper. Approximately how much money did the club gain, to the nearest thousand?

Write the (a) smallest and (b) largest possible number before it was rounded.

9 3700 rounded to the nearest hundred

10 75 000 rounded to the nearest thousand

11 4860 rounded to the nearest ten

12 469 000 rounded to the nearest thousand

13 58 700 rounded to the nearest hundred

14 47 390 rounded to the nearest ten

Rounding

These are the populations of different cities. Round each to the nearest thousand.

1. $|48,732 \rightarrow |49,000$

1 148 732   Huddersfield

2 154 917   Swindon

3 453 281   Liverpool

4 935 428   Birmingham

5 347 265   Leicester

6 462 842   Leeds

7 293 941   Cardiff

8 392 584   Manchester

9 679 325   Glasgow

Round each 4-digit number to the nearest 1000, and then use this to write an estimate.

10. $7 \times 3000 = 21,000$

10   7×2851

11   4132×3

12   $8721 - 3048$

13   $5239 + 3876$

14   $9172 \div 2$

15   $4886 \div 5$

16   $7231 + 4815 - 2940$

17   4×3861

18   1924×8

Explore

Use these cards. | 4 | 7 | 5 | 6 | 2 |

Create a 5-digit number. | 6 | 5 | 7 | 2 | 4 |

Round it to the nearest thousand.   *66 000*

Investigate how many different thousands you can create using these cards.

Rounding decimals

Write the position of each pointer, then round the number to (a) the nearest whole number, and (b) the nearest tenth.

1

c   e   a   d   b   f

4   5

2   k   g   i   l   j   h

26   27

These are the distances thrown in a 'welly wanging' competition. Round each distance to the nearest (a) whole number and (b) tenth.

3. 3 4·6 2 → a)3 5 m   b)3 4·6 m

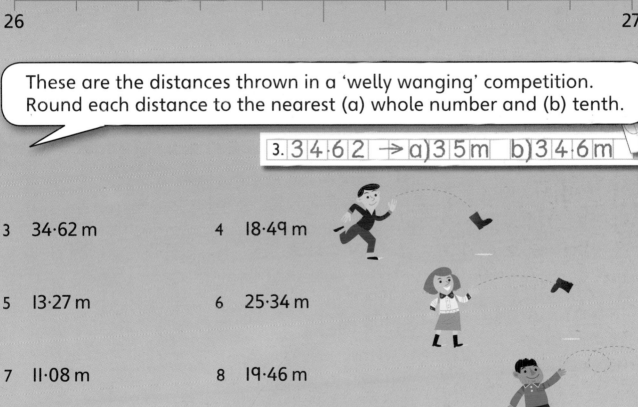

3 34·62 m	4 18·49 m	
5 13·27 m	6 25·34 m	
7 11·08 m	8 19·46 m	
9 26·23 m	10 42·39 m	11 20·06 m

If Jemma's throw rounded to the nearest whole metre was 24 m and Ricky's was 18 m, investigate the smallest and largest possible real difference between their distances.

Rounding decimals

These are the prices for train tickets. Round each price to the nearest (a) pound and (b) 10p.

1. £8·38 → a) £8 b) £8·40

1 Bodlington £8·38

2 Tarfield £14·52

3 Brookby £26·35

4 Dormouth £9·18

5 Jerby £32·41

6 Bottingham £18·76

7 Duxton £48·48

8 Backfield £32·91

9 Yutton £16·85

10 Wellstone £25·36

11 Bradby £17·18

12 Downscombe £42·67

If Su Li buys these two tickets, find the total cost, then round it to the nearest (a) pound and (b) 10p.

13 Jerby and Brookby

14 Tarfield and Backfield

15 Bodlington and Yutton

16 Bradby and Dormouth

17 Duxton and Wellstone

18 Downscombe and Bradby

19 Bottingham and Dormouth

20 Brookby and Backfield

21 Dormouth and Jerby

Are the answers the same if Su Li rounds both prices to the nearest pound first, then adds the two rounded amounts?

Rounding decimals

Create a number from each set of cards, then round it to the nearest (a) hundred, (b) ten, (c) whole number, (d) tenth.

1. 3 6 7 · 3 6 → a) 4 0 0 b) 3 7 0 c) ... d) ...

1 | 3 0 0 | | · 3 | | 7 |
   | 6 0 | | · 0 6 |

2 | · 5 | | 9 | | 9 0 0 |
   | · 0 6 |

3 | · 0 8 |
   | 8 | | · 6 |

4 | · 0 2 | | 6 |
   | 4 0 0 | | · 9 | | 4 0 |

Write the (a) smallest and (b) largest possible decimal number with two places before it was rounded:

5 8 rounded to the nearest whole number

6 48·3 rounded to the nearest tenth

7 35 rounded to the nearest whole number

8 40 rounded to the nearest ten

9 15·9 rounded to the nearest tenth

10 6·0 rounded to the nearest tenth

Explore

Use cards: | 4 | | 7 | | 5 | | 8 |

Arrange them to make a decimal number like this: | 7 | | 5 | · | 8 | | 4 |
Round it to the nearest whole number.
Investigate how many different rounded whole numbers you can find. Repeat for rounding to the nearest tenth.

9

Rounding decimals

Round each decimal number to the nearest whole number, and then use this to write an estimate.

1. $3 \times 10 = 30$

1	$3 \times 9 \cdot 72$	2	$6 \times 14 \cdot 35$	3	$44.71 - 14 \cdot 83$
4	$72 \cdot 35 + 17 \cdot 91$	5	$18 \cdot 72 \div 2$	6	$34 \cdot 67 \div 5$
7	$9 \cdot 72 + 8 \cdot 35 - 2 \cdot 89$	8	$4 \times 6 \cdot 83$	9	$14 \cdot 79 \times 6$

Estimate the perimeter of each garden by rounding.

10. $(2 \times 7) + (2 \times 6) = 14 + 12 = 26\,m$

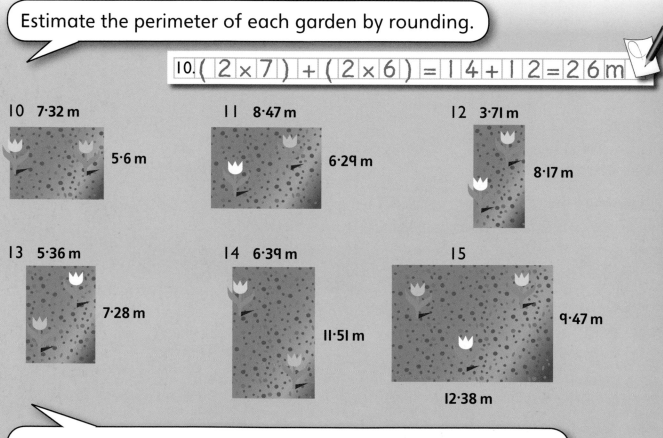

10 7·32 m
5·6 m

11 8·47 m
6·29 m

12 3·71 m
8·17 m

13 5·36 m
7·28 m

14 6·39 m
11·51 m

15
9·47 m
12·38 m

Estimate the area of each garden, and then use a calculator to calculate it accurately. Compare the two answers.

I have a square garden. I estimate that its area, when the length of its sides is rounded to the nearest metre, is 36 m². Use a calculator to investigate the smallest and largest possible accurate area.

Decimal numbers ✱

> Write the value of the underlined digits.

1. 4 tenths

1   1·4<u>2</u>   2   1·3<u>5</u>   3   2·67<u>4</u>

4   <u>8</u>·239   5   9·1<u>4</u>8   6   4·<u>2</u>57

7   3·06<u>8</u>   8   5·<u>7</u>04   9   11·29<u>1</u>

> Write each using numerals.

10.   3·75

10   three, seven tenths and five hundredths

11   four, two tenths, five hundredths and eight thousandths

12   six, seven tenths, nine hundredths and one thousandth

13   eight, three tenths, two hundredths and four thousandths

14   five, four hundredths and six thousandths

15   seven, two tenths and eight thousandths

16   three tenths, four hundredths and five thousandths

> Can you find some numbers like this (with units, tenths, hundredths and thousandths) that use 50 letters? How many?

> Write as a decimal number.

17   $4 + 0·3 + 0·05 + 0·007$ 18 $3 + 0·6 + 0·08 + 0·004$

19   $17 + 0·9 + 0·01 + 0·006$ 20 $25 + 0·04 + 0·003 + 0·1$

21   $12 + 0·009 + 0·2 + 0·06$ 22 $0·07 + 0·4 + 3 + 0·008$

23   $0·3 + 8 + 0·007$ 24 $0·002 + 9 + 0·04$

Decimal numbers

Write the numbers made by putting these cards together.

1.65487

1 | .007 | .08 | | 60 | .4 | 5

2 | 3 | .06 | 10 | .004 | .8

3 | 20 | .003 | .2 | 4 | .05

4 | 6 | .7 | .001 | 40

5 | 5 | .002 | 70 | .3

6 | 8 | .7 | .005 | .09 | 30

Write in order, smallest to largest:

7   8·6   8·59   8·593   8·581   8·602

8   4·514   4·451   4·145   4·541   4·415

9   0·38   0·385   0·358   0·35   0·4

10   2·17   2·183   2·18   2·174   2·147

11   3·1   3·085   3·09   3·092   3·04

Write a new number to fit between each of the numbers once you have ordered the lists above.

Decimal numbers

Write the distance hopped by each flea in (a) millimetres and (b) centimetres.

1. a)	1	7	3	2	m m	
b)	1	7	3	2	c m	

1   1·732 m

2   4·356 m

3   5·279 m

4   8·35 m

5   9·07 m

6   7·006 m

7   5·089 m

8   3·451 m

9   2·6 m

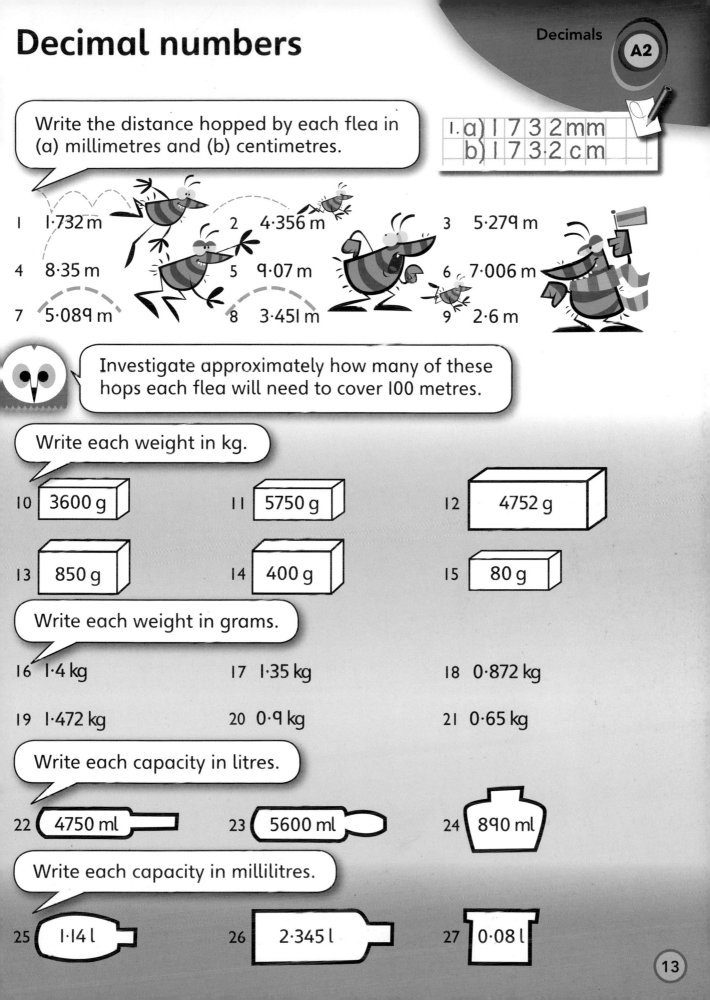

Investigate approximately how many of these hops each flea will need to cover 100 metres.

Write each weight in kg.

10   3600 g

11   5750 g

12   4752 g

13   850 g

14   400 g

15   80 g

Write each weight in grams.

16   1·4 kg

17   1·35 kg

18   0·872 kg

19   1·472 kg

20   0·9 kg

21   0·65 kg

Write each capacity in litres.

22   4750 ml

23   5600 ml

24   890 ml

Write each capacity in millilitres.

25   1·14 l

26   2·345 l

27   0·08 l

Decimal numbers

Write '<', '>' or '=' between each pair.

1·7 3 1 > 7·0 4

1 $7\frac{31}{100}$ 7·04   2 $5\frac{6}{10}$ 5·601

3 3·79   3·8   4 5·20   5·2

5 4·367   4·37   6 0·28   0·273

7 $\frac{146}{100}$ $\frac{15}{10}$ 8 3·142   3·124

9 12·435   12·453   10 8·014   8·13

Explore

Use the digits 7, 5, 0 and 4.

Make different decimal numbers with up to 3 decimal places.

Investigate how many different numbers you can make. Write them in order, smallest to largest.

Choose four digits of your own. Is the number of different numbers you can make the same?

Write a number that is exactly half-way between each pair.

11 4·2 ___ 4·3   12 5·46 ___ 5·48   13 2·32 ___ 2·33

14 4·274 ___ 4·278   15 6·34 ___ 6·346   16 19·28 ___ 19·4

17 5 ___ 5·082   18 8·3 ___ 8·246   19 7·12 ___ 7·194

2·56 is half-way between two numbers. What could they be if they are (a) both 2-place decimals, (b) both 3-place decimals, (c) one 2-place and one 3-place decimal?

Factors

Copy and complete each factor table to show all the pairs of factors of each number.

1 24

1	24
2	12
3	8

2 30

3 42

4 28

5 38

6 52

7 56

8 48

9 120

10 108

11 130

12 200

28 has three pairs of factors. There are three numbers less than 28 that have exactly three pairs of factors. Can you find them?

Write all the factor pairs of these numbers.

13. 8: 1 × 8, 2 × 4

13 8

14 12

15 20

16 40

17 53

18 26

19 18

20 39

Factors

Write a list of the factors of these numbers:

1. 14: 1, 2, 7, 14

1	14	2	22	3	24	4	30
5	34	6	44	7	45	8	56

True or false?

9   8 is a factor of 90   10   7 is a factor of 56   11   9 is a factor of 120

12   3 and 4 are both factors of 108   13   2 and 7 are both factors of 84

14   4 and 9 are both factors of 54   15   3 and 14 are both factors of 126

Each of these lists has a missing factor. Can you find it?

16 *factors of 45*   1, 3, 5, 15, 45

17 *factors of 36*   1, 2, 3, 4, 9, 12, 18, 36

18 *factors of 28*   1, 2, 4, 7, 28

19 *factors of 18*   1, 2, 3, 6, 18

20 *factors of 42*   1, 2, 3, 6, 7, 21, 42

21 *factors of 46*   1, 2, 46

22 *factors of 49*   1, 49

23 *factors of 54*   1, 2, 3, 6, 9, 27, 54

Can you create a list of factors of six different numbers, each with a missing factor of 9?

Factors

| 2 | 7 | 8 | q | 14 | 3 | 6 | 4 |

Which of these numbers are factors of:

1 52   2 58   3 64   4 70?

| 16 | 4 | 12 | 8 | 5 | 18 | q |

Which of these numbers are factors of:

5 36   6 72   7 60   8 90?

9 **Which of these numbers has an odd number of factors?**

| 30 | 27 | q | 14 | 50 | 25 | 64 | 72 | 16 | 33 |

Arrange the digit cards to make four 2-digit numbers so that each sentence is true. You can only use each card once.

10 [1] [2] [3] [4]
    [5] [6] [7] [8]

3 is a factor of ☐☐

4 is a factor of ☐☐

5 is a factor of ☐☐

6 is a factor of ☐☐

11 [2] [3] [4] [5]
    [6] [7] [8] [9]

7 is a factor of ☐☐

q is a factor of ☐☐

8 is a factor of ☐☐

5 is a factor of ☐☐

Explore

Use one set of cards 0–9. Can you create three sentences like this: ☐ is a factor of ☐☐. Can you do it without using the 1-digit card?

Factors

Two of the sentences in each set are wrong. Can you find them?

1   Between 50 and 60 inclusive:

Two numbers have only 2 factors.
Five numbers have 4 factors.
One number has 6 factors.
Two numbers have 8 factors.
No numbers have 10 factors.
One number has 12 factors.

2   Between 40 and 50 inclusive:

Three numbers have 2 factors.
One number has 3 factors.
One number has 4 factors.
Four numbers have 6 factors.
One number has 8 factors.
One number has 10 factors.

Arrange the digits in the boxes so that each digit is a factor of both its row heading and its column heading. Draw a large grid and use number cards to help.

3   Digits: 1, 2, 2, 3, 3, 4, 4, 5, 6

	20	12	6
12			
6			
20			

4   Digits: 2, 3, 3, 4, 4, 5, 5, 6, 6

	30	12	60
12			
30			
60			

5   Digits: 1, 2, 3, 4, 4, 5, 6, 7, 8

	16	30	28
24			
35			
24			

6   Digits: 3, 3, 3, 4, 4, 5, 6, 8, 9

	12	24	45
15			
36			
24			

Draw a grid of your own to fill in.

Multiplying

Copy each rectangle and write its area.

1.

	20	4
5	100	20

$100 + 20 = 120 \, cm^2$

1 24 cm, 5 cm

2 4 cm, 18 cm

3 23 cm, 7 cm

4 6 cm, 25 cm

5 5 cm, 13 cm

6 7 cm, 26 cm

7 4 cm, 19 cm

8 22 cm, 7 cm

9 6 cm, 17 cm

Use cards 0–9 to create □ x □□. What is the largest total you can make? What is the smallest?

10. $(4 \times 80) + (4 \times 1)$
$320 + 4 = 324$

Copy and complete.

10 $4 \times 81 =$

11 $5 \times 63 =$

12 $6 \times 52 =$

13 $3 \times 73 =$

14 $5 \times 28 =$

15 $6 \times 17 =$

16 $4 \times 27 =$

17 $8 \times 23 =$

18 $7 \times 38 =$

Multiplying

Copy and complete.

1. $(6 \times 50) + (6 \times 6)$
   $300 + 36 = 336$

1 $6 \times 56 = \square$

2 $8 \times 37 = \square$

3 $5 \times 78 = \square$

4 $7 \times 47 = \square$

5 $6 \times 64 = \square$

6 $7 \times 29 = \square$

7 $5 \times 23 = \square$

8 $11 \times 32 = \square$

9 $8 \times 34 = \square$

Write the total cost of the trip.

10. $(6 \times 60) + (6 \times 8)$
    $360 + 48 = £408$

10 Fly to Paris £68

Fly to **Paris**, £68

6 People

11 Fly to Rome £72

Fly to **Rome, £72**

8 People

12 Sail to Jersey £44

Sail to **Jersey, £44**

7 People

13 Cycle to Dublin £36

Cycle to **Dublin, £36**

7 People

14 Sail to Iona £64

Sail to **Iona, £64**

8 People

15 Fly to Seville £59

Fly to **Seville, £59**

6 People

16 Fly to Prague £22

Fly to **Prague, £22**

6 People

17 Sail to Calais £87

Sail to **Calais, £87**

8 People

18 Fly to Milan £145

Fly to **Milan, £145**

7 People

Work with a partner to create the ×21 table.

Multiplying

> Write the total amount of juice.

1. $(6 \times 4) + (6 \times 0.7)$
   $... + ...$

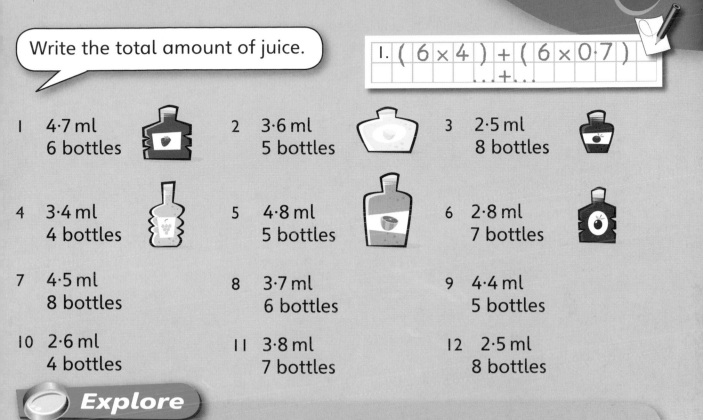

1.   4·7 ml
   6 bottles

2.   3·6 ml
   5 bottles

3.   2·5 ml
   8 bottles

4.   3·4 ml
   4 bottles

5.   4·8 ml
   5 bottles

6.   2·8 ml
   7 bottles

7.   4·5 ml
   8 bottles

8.   3·7 ml
   6 bottles

9.   4·4 ml
   5 bottles

10.   2·6 ml
    4 bottles

11.   3·8 ml
    7 bottles

12.   2·5 ml
    8 bottles

Explore

Use cards 0–9. Choose three cards to make a multiplication like this: ☐·☐ × ☐. Investigate how many different multiplications you can make that give an answer between 25 and 30.

13.   Kulpreet had 6 bags of sweets, each containing 64 assorted chocolates and fruit gums. How many sweets did she have in all? How many more to have 500?

14.   Mrs Bird bought 8 bags of peanuts, each with 56 nuts in, and 7 sacks of bird treats, each with 28 bird treats. How many peanuts and bird treats does she have?

15.   Matt's car uses 8·6 l of petrol to get to work. Matt works 6 days a week. How much petrol does he use? The cost of petrol is £1·10 per litre. How much money does Matt spend on petrol in 1 week?

Multiplying

Use the factors of the first number. Multiply the second number.

1. | 1 | 8 | × | 4 | 5 |
   |---|---|---|---|---|
   | 9 | × | 2 | × | 4 | 5 |
   | 9 | × | 9 | 0 | |
   | = | 8 | 1 | 0 | |

1   18 × 45 =

2   15 × 35 =

3   14 × 15 =

4   18 × 55 =

5   16 × 27 =

6   24 × 33 =

7   15 × 44 =

8   18 × 42 =

9   16 × 34 =

10   15 × 28 =

11   18 × 38 =

12   24 × 24 =

13   18 × 23 =

14   15 × 29 =

15   36 × 17 =

Find the number of glasses in each box.

16
15 rows
22 glasses per row

17
18 rows
25 glasses per row

18
21 rows
19 glasses per row

19
16 rows
23 glasses per row

20
17 rows
25 glasses per row

21
18 rows
24 glasses per row

22
19 rows
22 glasses per row

23
18 rows
23 glasses per row

24
16 rows
24 glasses per row

How could 480 glasses be arranged in a rectangular box?

Multiplying

Write out the ×10 and the ×2 tables.
Add the multiples.
Use the ×12 table to help you work out the answers!

10	20	30	40	...
2	4	6	8	...
12	24	36	...	...

1. $(12 \times 20) + (12 \times 3) =$
$240 + 36 = 276$

1   12 × 23

2   12 × 27

3   12 × 31

4   12 × 43

5   35 × 12

6   12 × 47

7   52 × 12

8   42 × 12

9   39 × 12

10 48 × 12

11 33 × 12

12 28 × 12

13   Omar had a favourite book. It was
26 pages long. He read it 15 times!
How many pages has he read?

Explore

Work out the ×13 table using the same method as shown above.

Use this table to help you multiply by 26.

What other multiplication facts can ×13 help with?
For example, ×39 or ×52.

Explore writing some really big multiplications, e.g. 8 × 52.

Multiplying

Write out the ×10 and ×4 tables. Add these to get the ×14 table. Use this to help you complete the multiplications.

10	20	30	40	...
4	8	12	16	...
14	28	...		

1. $(14 \times 20) + (14 \times 7) =$
$280 + 98 = 378$

1	14×27	2	14×36	3	14×23
4	14×38	5	42×14	6	53×14
7	34×14	8	45×14	9	24×28

Find some big square numbers, e.g. 14×14, 18×18, 17×17.

All these ice-creams cost 13p. Work out the total prices.

HINT: Work out the ×13 table. Use it to help you.

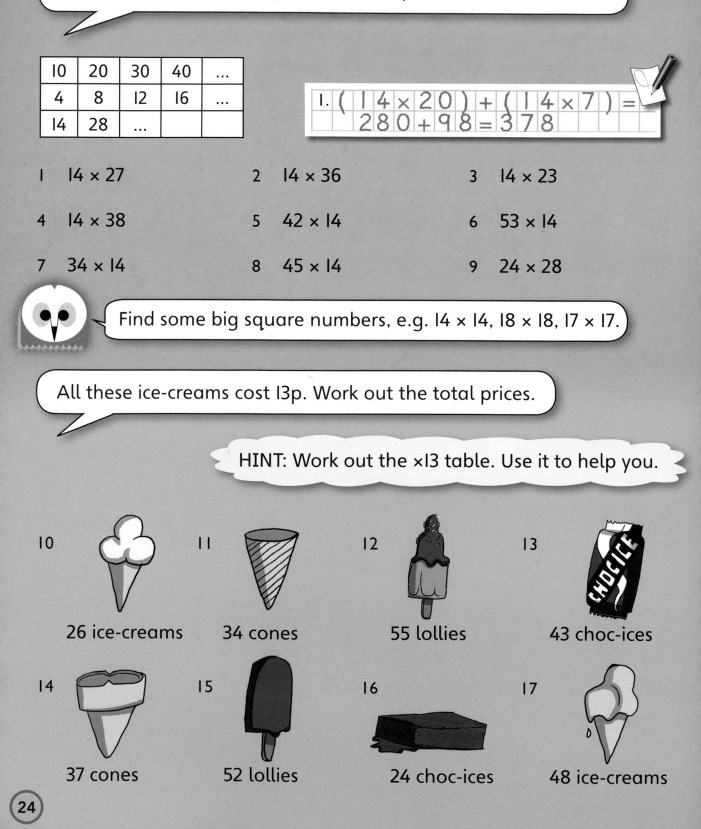

10   26 ice-creams

11   34 cones

12   55 lollies

13   43 choc-ices

14   37 cones

15   52 lollies

16   24 choc-ices

17   48 ice-creams

Multiplying

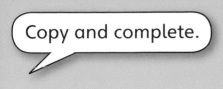

Copy and complete.

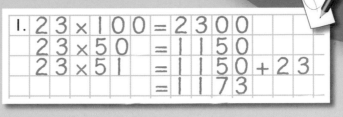

```
1. 23 × 100 = 2300
   23 × 50  = 1150
   23 × 51  = 1150 + 23
            = 1173
```

1   23 × 51

2   52 × 76

3   99 × 43

4   101 × 64

5   51 × 38

6   52 × 73

7   Hani is 26 years old. How many weeks until he has lived 1500 weeks?

8   Jason scores 23 points in each match and he plays 49 matches in a season. How many points does he score?

9   Parvati has 13 shots on target each game and she plays 52 games. How many shots on target does she have in all?

Oranges are packed in boxes of 49. Write the total number of oranges.

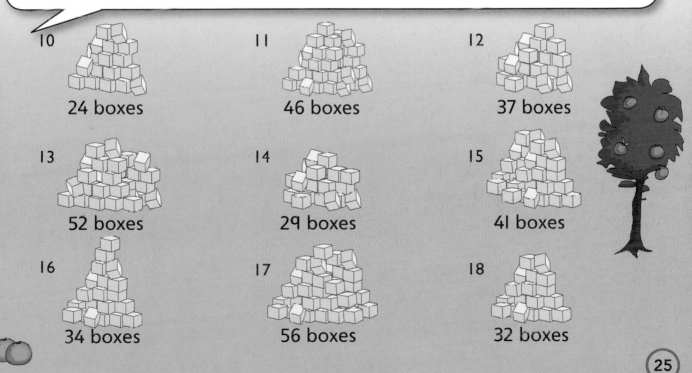

10   24 boxes

11   46 boxes

12   37 boxes

13   52 boxes

14   29 boxes

15   41 boxes

16   34 boxes

17   56 boxes

18   32 boxes

Multiplying

Choose a method to suit each calculation.

17 × 63
Use × 17 table

18 × 55
Use factors

23 × 49
Use rounding

1 17 × 63

2 18 × 55

3 23 × 49

4 15 × 73

5 17 × 54

6 35 × 35

7 18 × 67

8 13 × 82

9 124 × 12

10 236 × 11

11 42 × 49

12 16 × 46

13 28 × 75

14 24 × 43

15 49 × 123

16 49 × 68

17 14 × 37

18 18 × 48

Explore

Does 12 × 42 = 21 × 24?
Try 12 × 84 = 21 × 48.
Now try 13 × 62 and 31 × 26.
Can you find another pair of multiplications like these?

Coordinates

1   Write the coordinates of each point.

1. A (1 , 2)

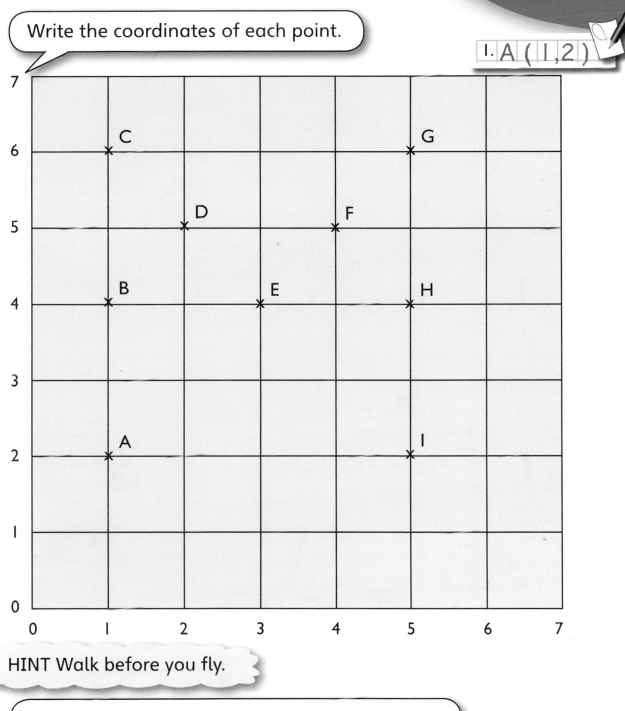

HINT Walk before you fly.

2   Copy this grid. Copy all the points. Join them to make a letter of the alphabet.

Plot four points. Join them to make different shapes, e.g. a 'butterfly' or a 'diamond'.

Coordinates

1 Write the coordinates of each point.

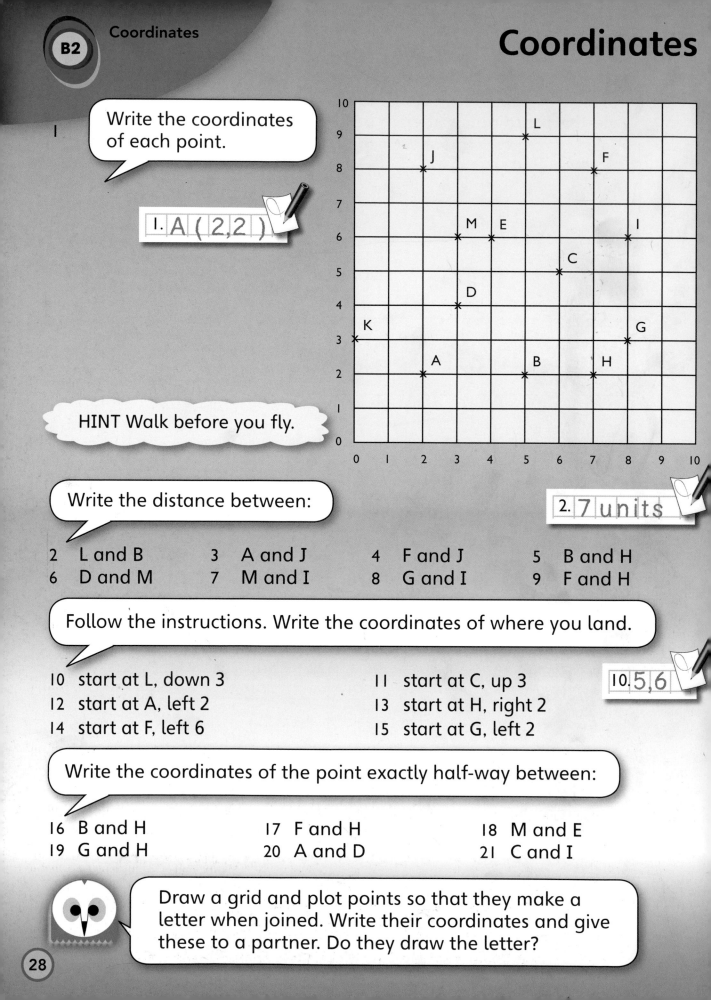

1. A (2,2)

HINT Walk before you fly.

2. 7 units

Write the distance between:

2 L and B	3 A and J	4 F and J	5 B and H
6 D and M	7 M and I	8 G and I	9 F and H

Follow the instructions. Write the coordinates of where you land.

10. 5,6

10 start at L, down 3	11 start at C, up 3
12 start at A, left 2	13 start at H, right 2
14 start at F, left 6	15 start at G, left 2

Write the coordinates of the point exactly half-way between:

16 B and H	17 F and H	18 M and E
19 G and H	20 A and D	21 C and I

Draw a grid and plot points so that they make a letter when joined. Write their coordinates and give these to a partner. Do they draw the letter?

Coordinates

1 Write the coordinates of each point.

1. A (1 , 1)

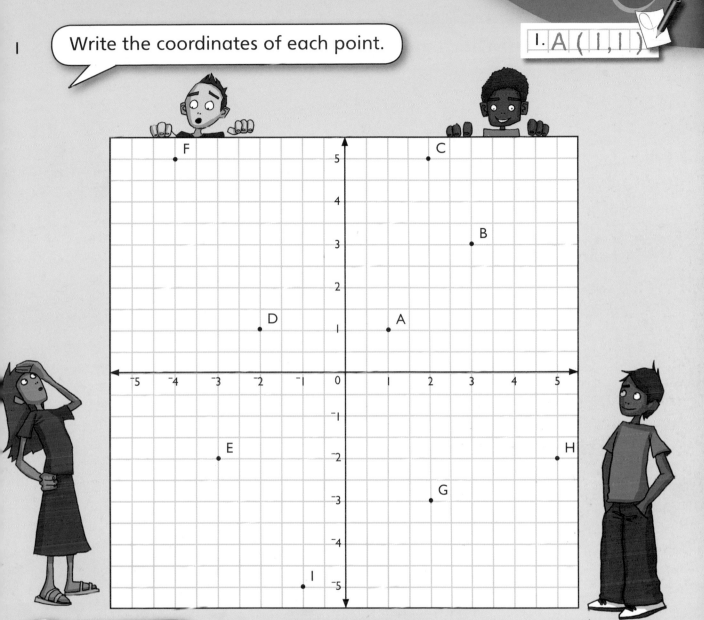

Explore

Draw two axes.

Plot four points in the first quadrant. Join the points to make a shape.

Reflect your shape in the x-axis.

Write the new coordinates. What do you notice?

Reflect your shape in the y-axis. What do you notice about the coordinates now?

3D shapes

Write the name of each shape. How many faces does it have?

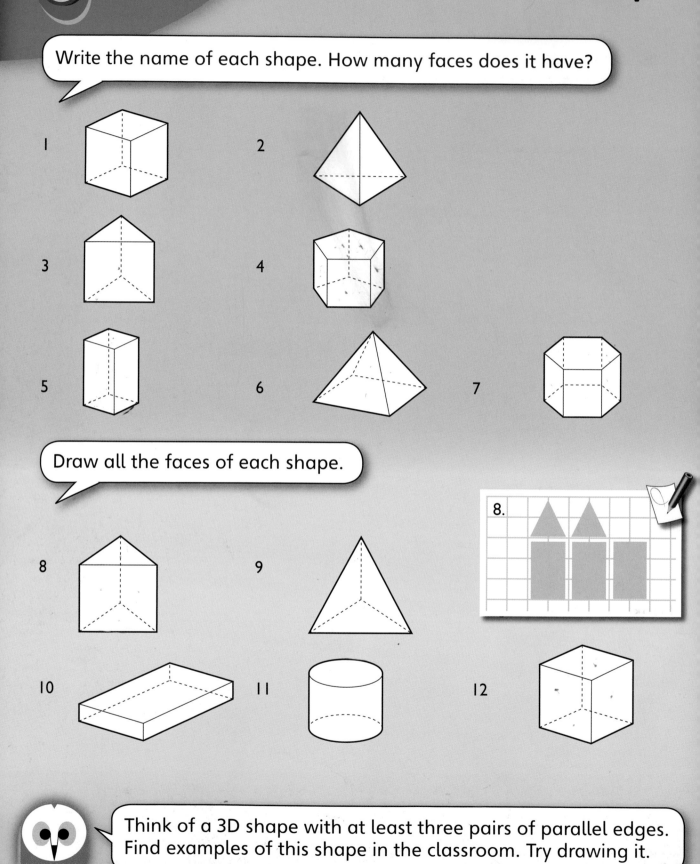

1

2

3

4

5

6

7

Draw all the faces of each shape.

8

9

8.

10

11

12

Think of a 3D shape with at least three pairs of parallel edges. Find examples of this shape in the classroom. Try drawing it.

3D shapes

> Write the name of each shape. Count the faces. Draw each different face and name it. Say how many there are.

1. Cuboid
   6 faces

   ×2   ×2   ×2
   rectangle rectangle rectangle

1

2

3

4

5

6

| hexagonal prism | octahedron | tetrahedron | square-based pyramid |

> Look at each shape. Does it have:

1. a) yes
   b) ...

a   parallel faces
c   perpendicular edges

b   perpendicular faces
d   parallel edges?

Explore

Can you think of (and draw) a 3D shape with an odd number of faces and at least one pair of parallel edges?

Can you find more than one shape like this?

3D shapes

Look at each shape. Build it from cubes. Write the number of faces.

1. 6 faces

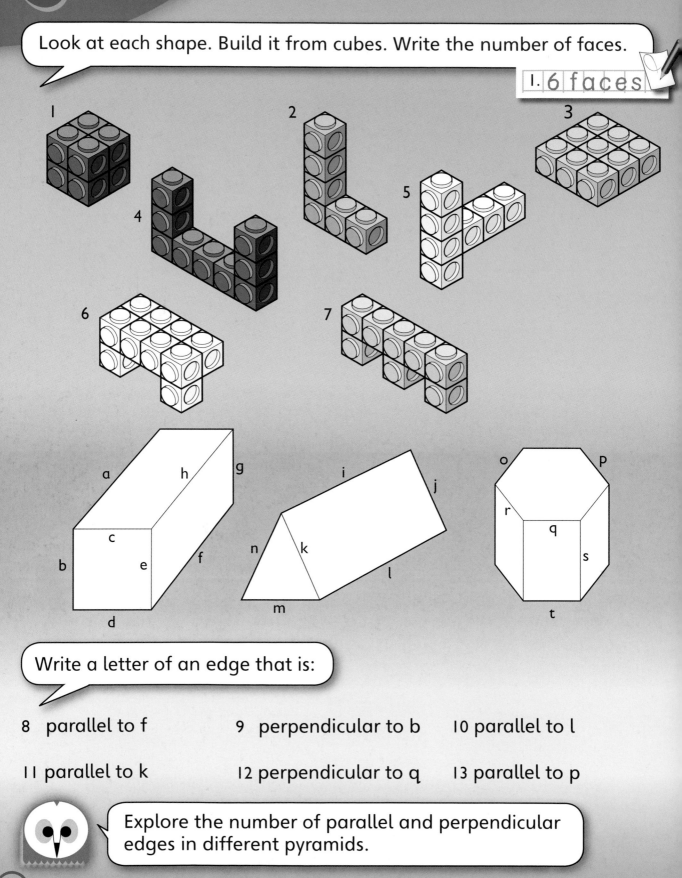

1   2   3

4   5

6   7

a h g
c
b e f
d

i j
n k
m l

o p
r
q
s
t

Write a letter of an edge that is:

8   parallel to f   9   perpendicular to b   10 parallel to l

11 parallel to k   12 perpendicular to q   13 parallel to p

Explore the number of parallel and perpendicular edges in different pyramids.

3D shapes

Write the name of the shape made by each net. Write 'none' if it is impossible!

1. cube

1

2

3

4

5

6

7

8

9

True or false?

10 A cuboid has three pairs of parallel faces.

11 A cube always has six identical faces.

12 A square-based pyramid has no perpendicular edges.

13 A dodecahedron has more than 12 faces.

14 A cuboid is a type of prism.

15 A tetrahedron has one pair of parallel faces.

16 A hexagonal prism has more than three pairs of parallel edges.

17 A regular octahedron has eight faces that are equilateral triangles.

Area of rectangles

Calculate the areas of these rectangles.

1. Area = 5 × 3
       = 15 cm²

1 5 cm, 3 cm

2 4 cm, 6 cm

3 12 cm, 7 cm

4 7.5 m, 8 m

5 30 mm, 20 mm

6 3.5 cm, 10 cm

Investigate the length and width of rectangles, in cm, that have an area of 1200 mm².

Find the total shaded area.

7 3 m, 5 m, 2 m, 3 m, 5 m

8 3 m, 5 m, 4 m, 12 m

9 11 m, 4 m, 9 m, 6 m

10 12 m, 7 m, 16 m, 7 m

11 3 m, 8 m, 14 m, 20 m

12 13 m, 30 m, 25 m, 40 m

Calculate the perimeter of each shape.

Area of rectangles

Write these areas in different units.

1. $1 cm^2 = 10 \times 10 = 100 mm^2$

1	1 cm² in mm²	2	1 m² in cm²	3	7 cm² in mm²
4	4000 mm² in cm²	5	4·5 m² in cm²	6	60 000 cm² in mm²
7	1 km² in m²	8	35 cm² in mm²	9	4 000 000 mm² in cm²

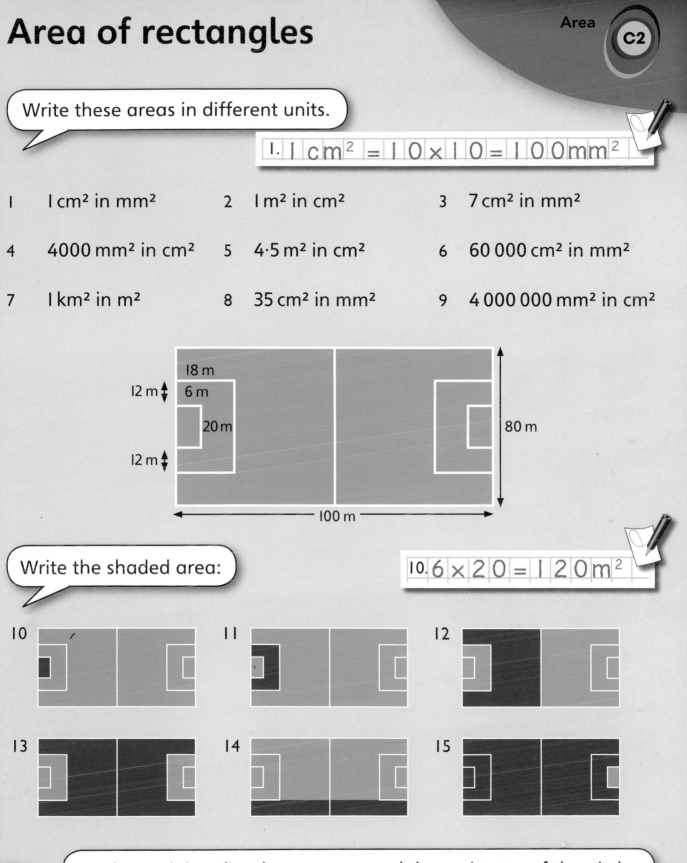

Write the shaded area:

10. $6 \times 20 = 120 m^2$

10   11   12

13   14   15

During training the players run round the perimeter of the pitch. Investigate how far they run for different numbers of laps of the pitch. How many laps are needed to run 21 km, 5 km, 10 km?

Area of rectangles

Calculate the area of the side of each bridge.

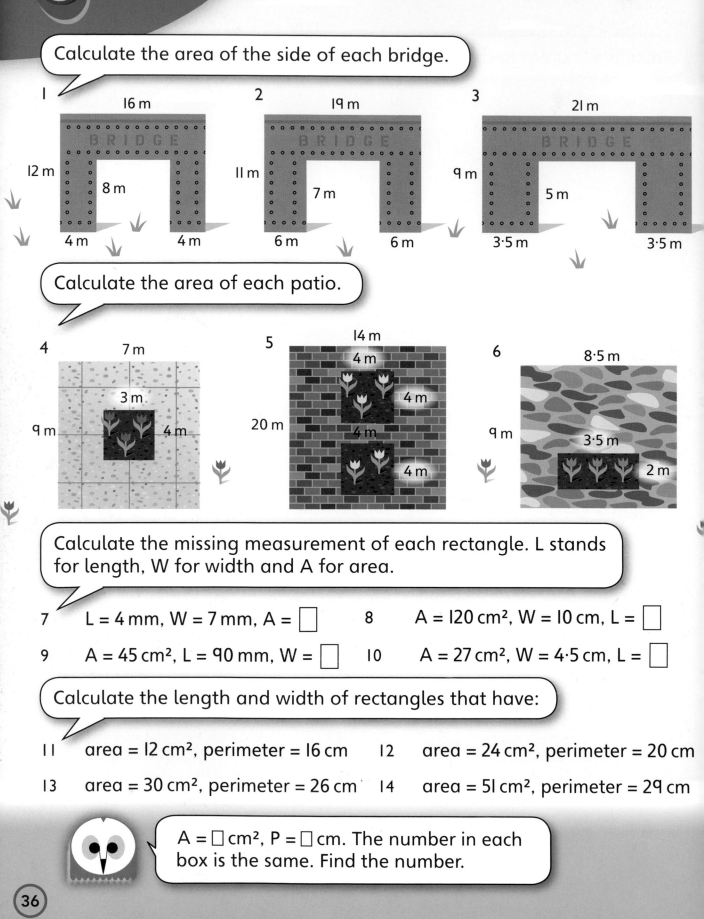

1   16 m
    12 m
    8 m
    4 m   4 m

2   19 m
    11 m
    7 m
    6 m   6 m

3   21 m
    9 m
    5 m
    3·5 m   3·5 m

Calculate the area of each patio.

4   7 m
    9 m
    3 m
    4 m

5   14 m
    4 m
    20 m
    4 m
    4 m
    4 m

6   8·5 m
    9 m
    3·5 m
    2 m

Calculate the missing measurement of each rectangle. L stands for length, W for width and A for area.

7   L = 4 mm, W = 7 mm, A = ☐

8   A = 120 cm², W = 10 cm, L = ☐

9   A = 45 cm², L = 90 mm, W = ☐

10   A = 27 cm², W = 4·5 cm, L = ☐

Calculate the length and width of rectangles that have:

11   area = 12 cm², perimeter = 16 cm

12   area = 24 cm², perimeter = 20 cm

13   area = 30 cm², perimeter = 26 cm

14   area = 51 cm², perimeter = 29 cm

A = ☐ cm², P = ☐ cm. The number in each box is the same. Find the number.

Surface area of cuboids

Calculate the surface area of each box.

I. $(2 \times 9) + (2 \times 15) + (2 \times 15) = ...$

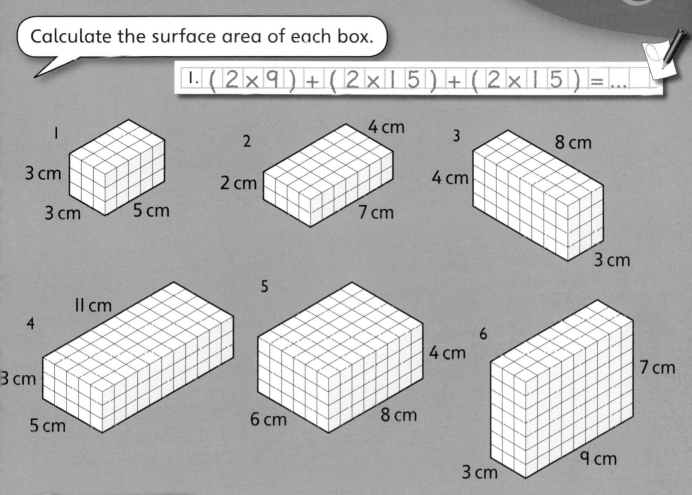

1 3 cm 3 cm 5 cm

2 4 cm 2 cm 7 cm

3 8 cm 4 cm 3 cm

4 11 cm 3 cm 5 cm

5 4 cm 6 cm 8 cm

6 7 cm 3 cm 9 cm

Explore

Use five cubes of the same size.

Make different models by joining them face to face.

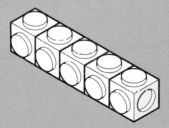
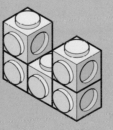

Investigate the surface areas of the models. Is it always the same? If not, what are the smallest and largest surface areas?

Now try this using six cubes.

Area of right-angled triangles

Calculate the area of the shaded triangle.

1. 6 × 8 = 48
   Area = 24 cm²

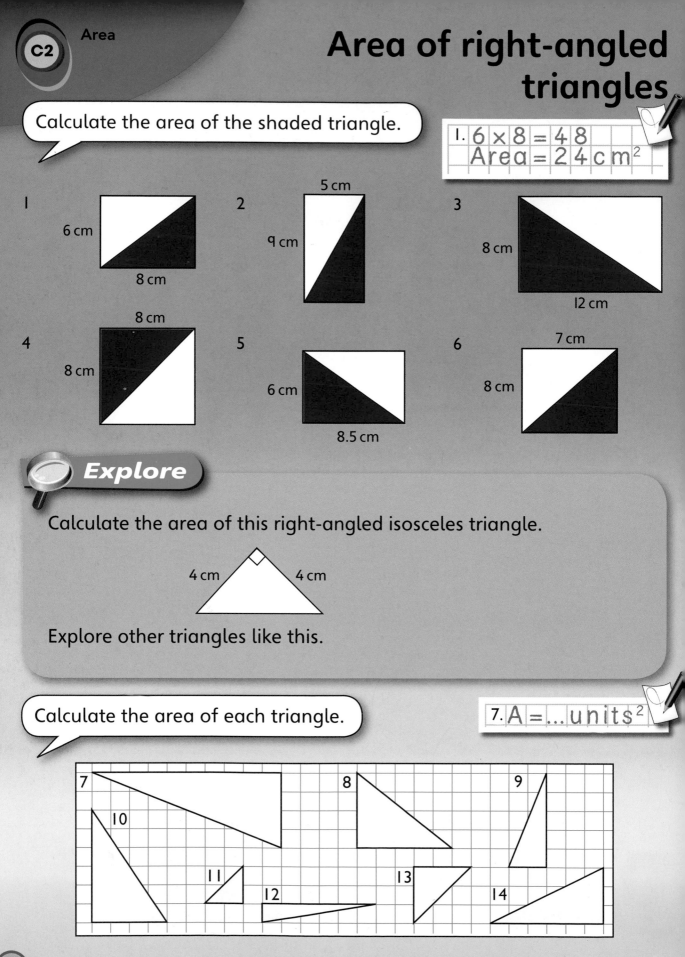

1   6 cm   8 cm

2   5 cm   9 cm

3   8 cm   12 cm

4   8 cm   8 cm

5   6 cm   8.5 cm

6   7 cm   8 cm

Explore

Calculate the area of this right-angled isosceles triangle.

4 cm   4 cm

Explore other triangles like this.

Calculate the area of each triangle.

7. A = ... units²

7   10   11   12   8   13   9   14

Area of right-angled triangles

On squared paper, draw a right-angled triangle with these areas. Start by drawing a rectangle.

1   12 cm²   2   28 cm²   3   15 cm²   4   7·5 cm²

Calculate the area of the side of each wedge.

5. 5 × 6 = 30
   Area = 15 cm²

5   5 cm
    6 cm

6   4 cm
    7 cm

7   6.5 cm
    8 cm

8   10 cm
    12 cm

9   7 cm
    9 cm

10   6 cm
     13 cm

Calculate the surface area of each wedge.

11   5 cm   2 cm
             3 cm
     4 cm

12   6 cm   10 cm
     3 cm
        8 cm

13   13 cm
     7 cm   5 cm
          12 cm

Explore

A right-angled triangle has an area of 36 cm².

Investigate possible lengths of its sides which form the right-angle.

Now try this with a triangle with an area of 40 cm².

Area of shapes that contain right-angled triangles

Find the areas of these shapes.

1. A = 2 cm²

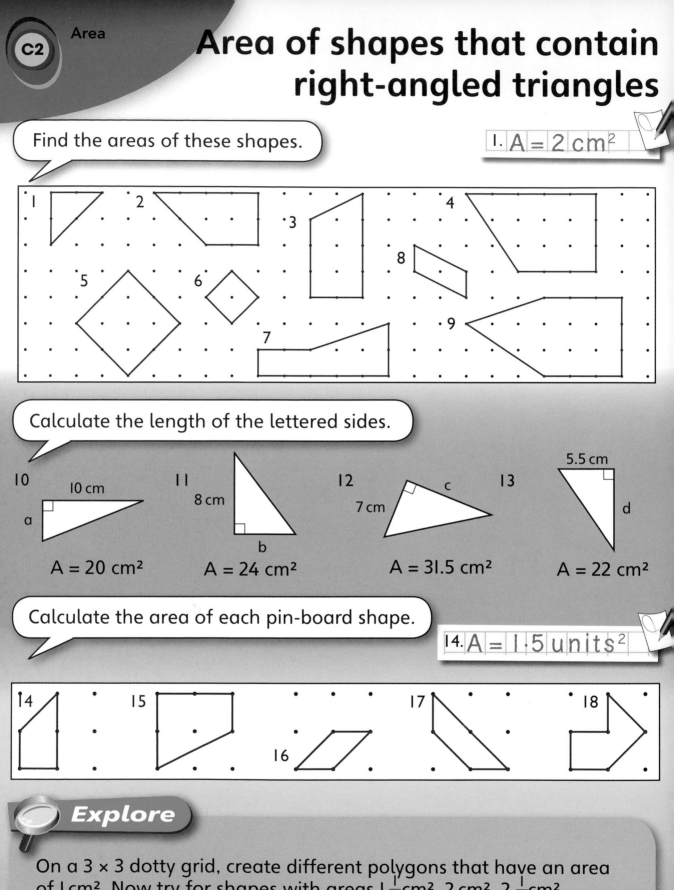

Calculate the length of the lettered sides.

10   10 cm   a   A = 20 cm²

11   8 cm   b   A = 24 cm²

12   7 cm   c   A = 31.5 cm²

13   5.5 cm   d   A = 22 cm²

Calculate the area of each pin-board shape.

14. A = 1.5 units²

14   15   16   17   18

Explore

On a 3 × 3 dotty grid, create different polygons that have an area of 1 cm². Now try for shapes with areas 1$\frac{1}{2}$cm², 2 cm², 2$\frac{1}{2}$cm², ..., 4 cm². How many of each can you create?

Area of non right-angled triangles

Calculate the areas of these non right-angled triangles by splitting them into two right-angled triangles.

$1.4 \times 8 = 32$
$A = 16 + 16 = 32 \text{ cm}^2$

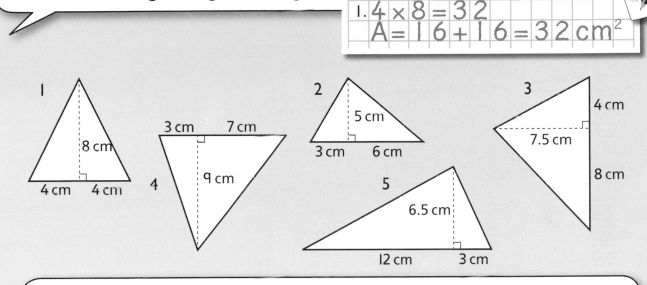

6   Ruth thinks of a rectangle that has a length of 12 cm and a width of 8 cm. Both diagonals are drawn to create four triangles. Can you find the areas of the four triangles?

Explore

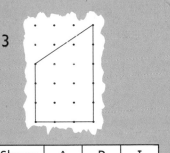

Draw these polygons on squared dotty paper. For each polygon, write:

- its area (A)
- the number of dots on the perimeter (P)
- the number of inside dots (I)

Shape	A	P	I
1			
2			
3			

Investigate a relationship between A, P and I.
Try other polygons.

Averages

Calculate the mean of each set of numbers.

1. $6 + 8 = 14$
   $14 \div 2 = 7$

1   6   8

2   7   9

3   8   5

4   4   5   6

5   7   10   4

6   3   6   9

7   3   5   5   7

8   4   6   11   3

9   5   10   7   6

Calculate the mean number of letters in the names of each set.

10. $6 + 4 + 8 = \dots$
    $\dots \div 3 = \dots$

10   Claire   Ruth   Caroline

11   Tom   Ben   Kate   Chang

12   Stephen   Patrick   Richard

13   Davinder   Elizabeth

14   Lucy   Ahmed   Harriet   Sean

15   Tanya   Sam   Jamal   Gary   Callum

Investigate the mean number of letters in a set of the names of yourself and friends.

Averages

Each player in a team took 10 penalties. These are the number of goals scored. Calculate the mean number of goals scored by the players in each team.

1. Reds: 5, 7, 4, 7, 7

> 1. Reds: $5 + 7 + 4 + 7 + 7 = ...$
> $... \div 5 ...$

2. Yellows: 8, 2, 7, 4, 4

3. Maroons: 3, 2, 5, 4, 4, 6

4. Greys: 8, 7, 7, 6

5. Whites: 6, 10, 8, 9, 9, 9, 5

6. Greens: 4, 3, 6, 5, 5, 7

7. Stripes: 6, 6, 8, 7, 9, 6

Which team is the best at taking penalties?
For each team write (a) the mode and (b) the range of goals scored.

In a football-juggling competition, each player had 10 attempts to see how many times they could keep the ball in the air. Calculate the mean score for each player.

> 8. $2 + 1 + 3 = ...$

8. Dan   2, 1, 3, 7, 4, 6, 5, 8, 2, 1

9. Ramesh   4, 3, 4, 2, 3, 4, 2, 3, 4, 2

10. Peter   6, 6, 3, 6, 3, 6, 7, 10, 7, 3

11. Cho   9, 9, 2, 8, 12, 10, 3, 3, 6, 10

12. Beth   4, 4, 8, 10, 4, 3, 6, 9, 2, 7

13. Guy   12, 15, 11, 12, 22, 13, 12, 9, 11, 15

Write the players in order, based on their mean scores.

Investigate some different possible sets of 10 scores if the mean is 6·5.

Averages

The children in Class 6 are collecting tokens.
The data shows how many they collect each week.
Calculate the median number collected by each child.

1. 1, 1, 2, 3, ...
   Median = ...

1 Tracey 4, 7, 3, 1, 2, 3, 4, 5, 1

2 Afram 1, 2, 1, 2, 3, 4, 5

3 Chrissie 2, 5, 3, 5, 2, 3, 4, 1

4 Hema 6, 7, 4, 6, 3, 8, 2, 2, 1, 9

5 Josh 3, 2, 1, 4, 2, 1, 3, 4

6 Nathan 5, 5, 5, 5, 3, 2, 5, 6, 7, 9, 5

Calculate the mean number collected by
each child. Write it as a mixed number.

Explore

Use this set of cards:

| 4 | 5 | 6 | 7 | 8 |
| 4 | 5 | 6 | 7 | 8 |

Investigate different sets of digits that have a mean of 6.

5 7   mean = 6   6 6 4 8   mean = 6

How many sets can you find?

Now try sets that have mean of 5 and sets that have a mean of 7.

Averages

Explore

Investigate the mean number of days per month in a year.
Find the median and mode and compare the three averages.
Do they change if it is a leap year?

These are the temperatures in °C for the first 10 days
in December. For each city, calculate (a) the mean, (b) the mode
and (c) the median temperature.

1   London 7, 7, 6, 5, 5, 7, 8, 7, 7, 6

2   Edinburgh 8, 8, 6, 6, 4, 5, 6, 7, 6, 6

3   Athens 18, 18, 20, 20, 19, 18, 17, 19, 21, 21

4   Barcelona 12, 12, 13, 14, 13, 13, 12, 12, 12, 13

5   Dublin 7, 6, 6, 7, 6, 5, 6, 7, 7, 8

6   Bordeaux 10, 12, 12, 11, 10, 11, 12, 13, 12, 12

7   Singapore 28, 28, 27, 28, 28, 27, 26, 28, 29, 28

8   Sydney 38, 36, 35, 36, 35, 33, 34, 33, 33, 32

Calculate the missing number in each set of cards.

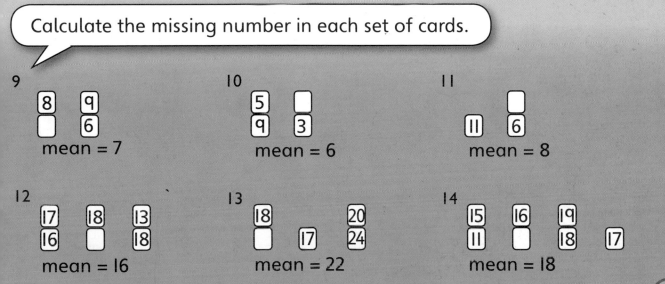

9

| 8 | 9 |
| ☐ | 6 |

mean = 7

10

| 5 | ☐ |
| 9 | 3 |

mean = 6

11

| | ☐ |
| 11 | 6 |

mean = 8

12

| 17 | 18 | 13 |
| 16 | ☐ | 18 |

mean = 16

13

| 18 | | 20 |
| ☐ | 17 | 24 |

mean = 22

14

| 15 | 16 | 19 | |
| 11 | ☐ | 18 | 17 |

mean = 18

Line graphs

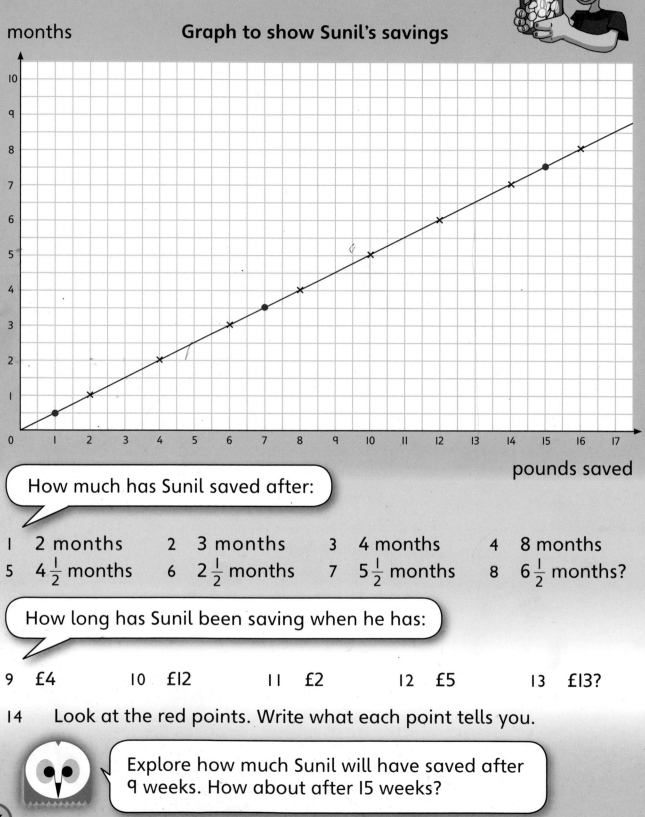

months

Graph to show Sunil's savings

pounds saved

How much has Sunil saved after:

1 2 months	2 3 months	3 4 months	4 8 months
5 $4\frac{1}{2}$ months	6 $2\frac{1}{2}$ months	7 $5\frac{1}{2}$ months	8 $6\frac{1}{2}$ months?

How long has Sunil been saving when he has:

9 £4   10 £12   11 £2   12 £5   13 £13?

14 Look at the red points. Write what each point tells you.

Explore how much Sunil will have saved after
9 weeks. How about after 15 weeks?

Line graphs

Annie sells candles at £5 for 10. Study the line graph of her sales.

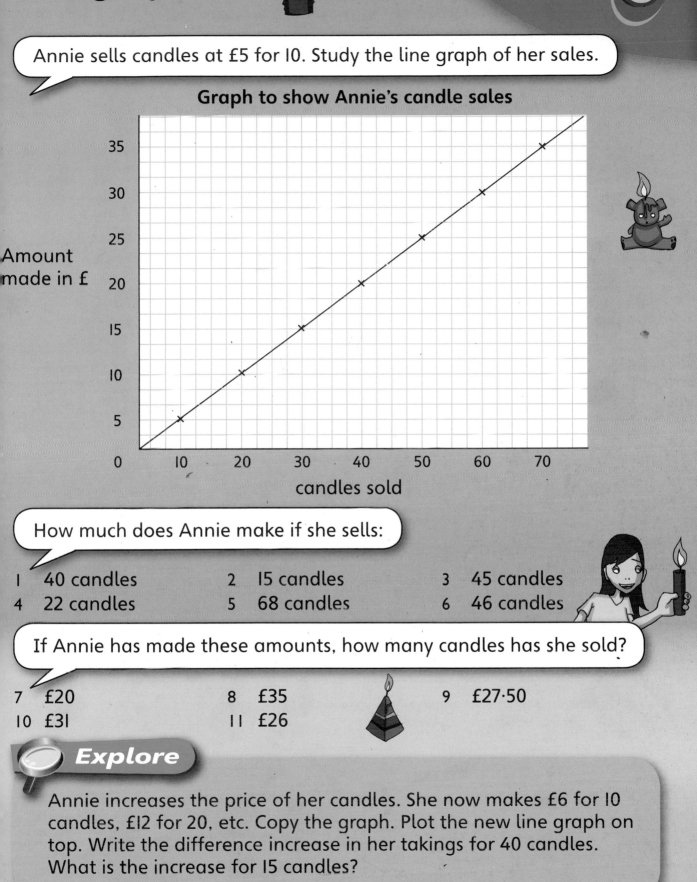

Graph to show Annie's candle sales

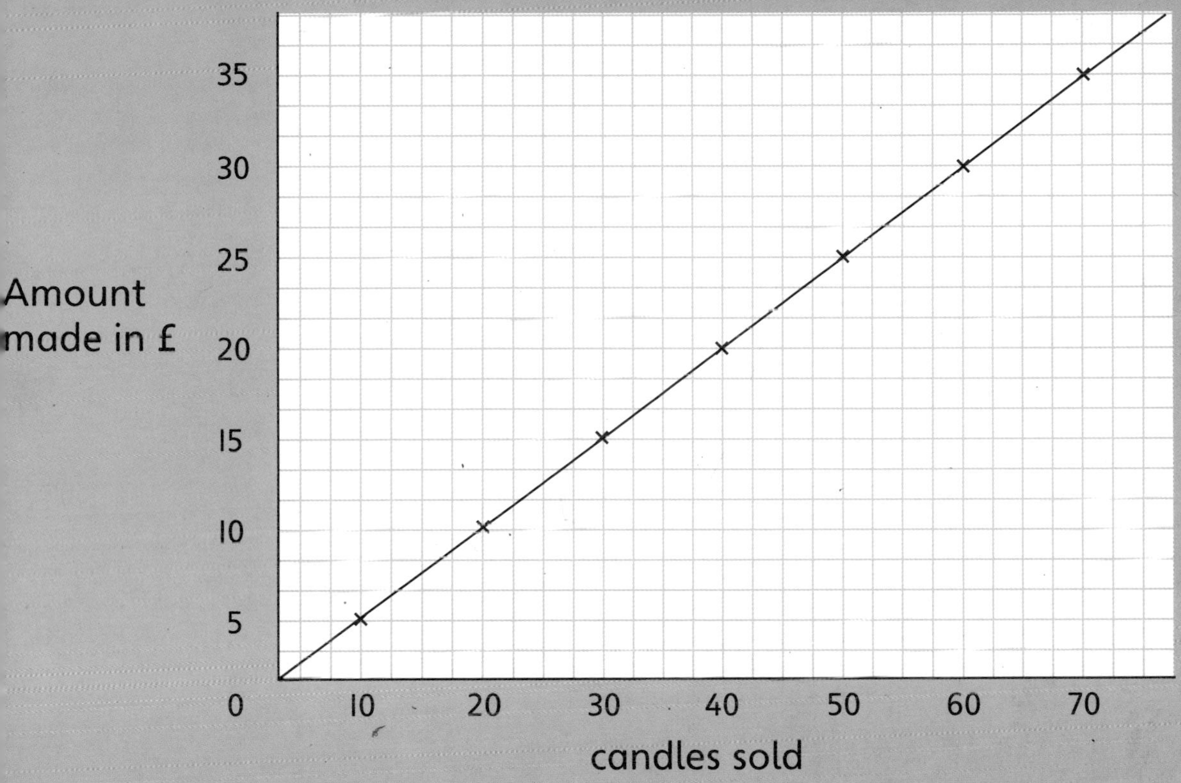

How much does Annie make if she sells:

1 40 candles
2 15 candles
3 45 candles
4 22 candles
5 68 candles
6 46 candles

If Annie has made these amounts, how many candles has she sold?

7 £20
8 £35
9 £27·50
10 £31
11 £26

Explore

Annie increases the price of her candles. She now makes £6 for 10 candles, £12 for 20, etc. Copy the graph. Plot the new line graph on top. Write the difference increase in her takings for 40 candles. What is the increase for 15 candles?

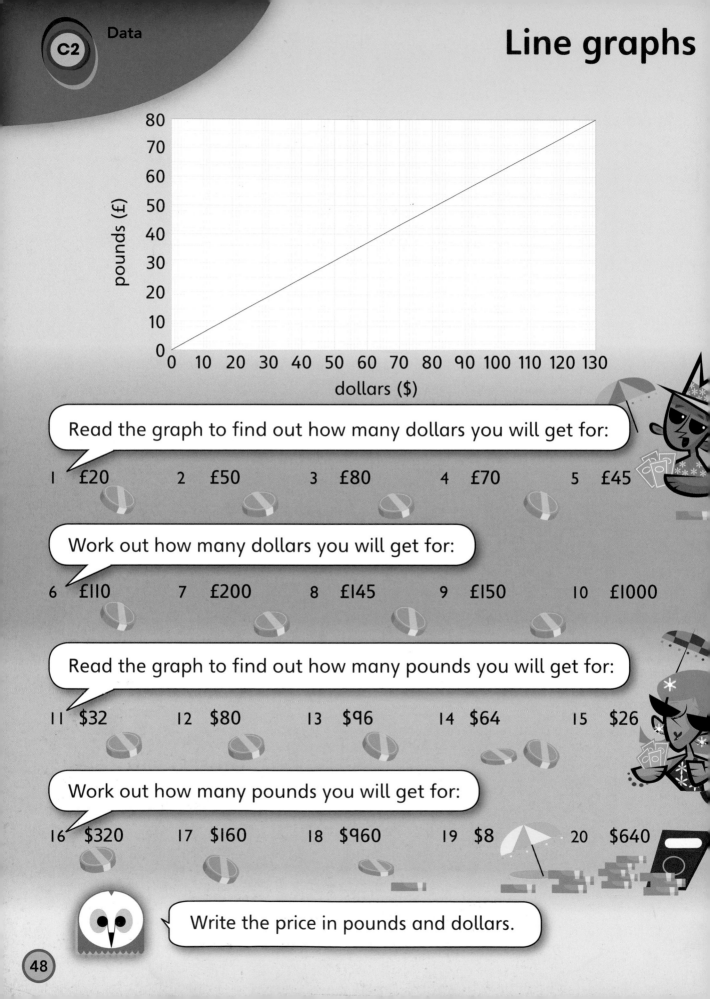

dollars ($)

Read the graph to find out how many dollars you will get for:

1 £20   2 £50   3 £80   4 £70   5 £45

Work out how many dollars you will get for:

6 £110   7 £200   8 £145   9 £150   10 £1000

Read the graph to find out how many pounds you will get for:

11 $32   12 $80   13 $96   14 $64   15 $26

Work out how many pounds you will get for:

16 $320   17 $160   18 $960   19 $8   20 $640

Write the price in pounds and dollars.

Line graphs

Copy the table and extend it up to £10. Draw a line graph marking the horizontal axis up to £10. Use the graph to convert the prices!

x-axis (£)	1	2	3	4
y-axis (Rupees)	80	160	240	

1   800 R

2   240 R

3   440 R

4   480 R

5   360 R

6   1600 R

7   1200 R

8   4000 R

9   200 R

How much will Hilda get in rupees for:

10 £3   11 £5   12 £10   13 £2·50

14 £15   15 £7·50   16 £40

Explore the amount in pounds if you have 1 million rupees. Estimate first with your partner.

Adding and subtracting

Write how much is left in the purse.

1. £3·55 − 40p = £3·15

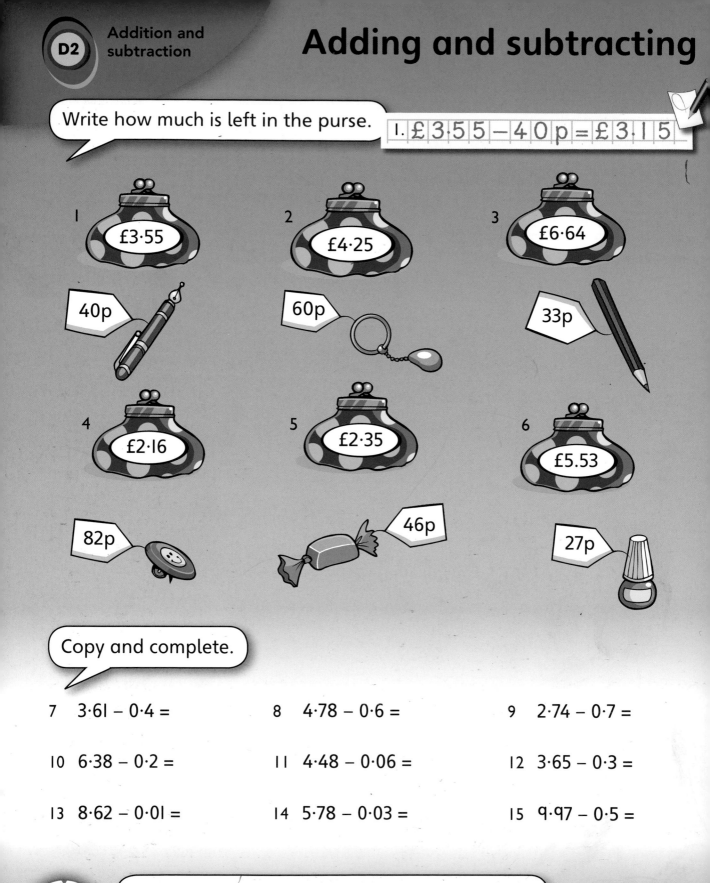

1. £3·55 — 40p
2. £4·25 — 60p
3. £6·64 — 33p
4. £2·16 — 82p
5. £2·35 — 46p
6. £5.53 — 27p

Copy and complete.

7   3·61 − 0·4 =

8   4·78 − 0·6 =

9   2·74 − 0·7 =

10   6·38 − 0·2 =

11   4·48 − 0·06 =

12   3·65 − 0·3 =

13   8·62 − 0·01 =

14   5·78 − 0·03 =

15   9·97 − 0·5 =

How many different digits can fill the missing numbers in this addition? $4 \cdot \square 1 + 0 \cdot \square 9 = 5$

Adding and subtracting

Copy and complete.

1. $0.7 + 0.46 = 1.16$

1	$0.7 + 0.46 =$	2	$0.5 + 0.72 =$
3	$0.6 + 0.55 =$	4	$0.4 + 0.61 =$
5	$0.5 + 0.64 =$	6	$0.7 + 0.53 =$
7	$0.6 + 0.82 =$	8	$0.4 + 0.76 =$

Write how much ribbon is left.

9. $0.53 - 0.2 = 0.33$

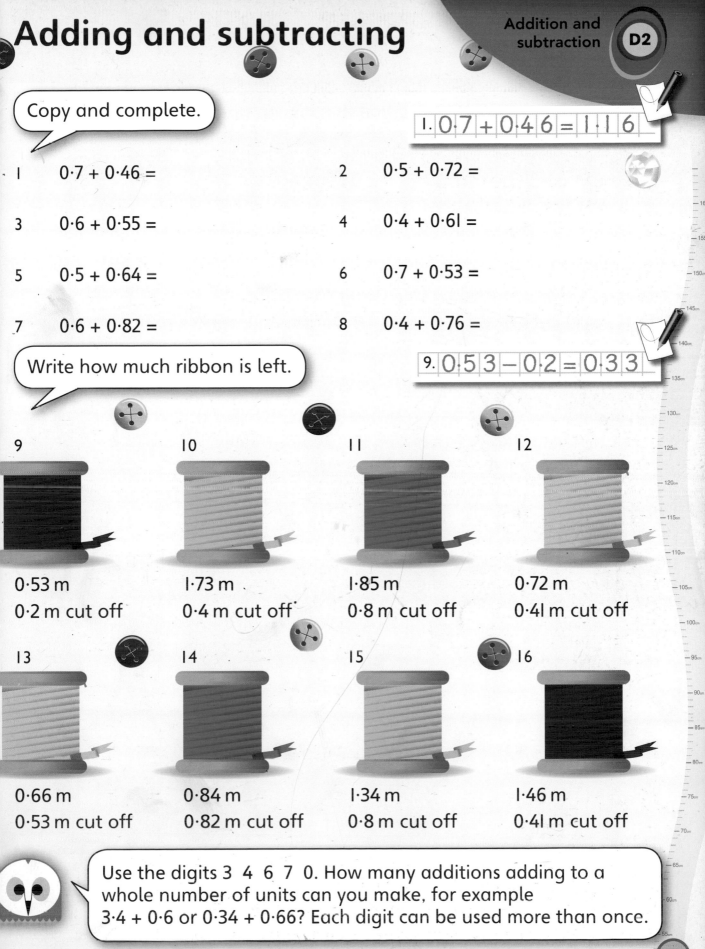

9
0·53 m
0·2 m cut off

10
1·73 m
0·4 m cut off

11
1·85 m
0·8 m cut off

12
0·72 m
0·41 m cut off

13
0·66 m
0·53 m cut off

14
0·84 m
0·82 m cut off

15
1·34 m
0·8 m cut off

16
1·46 m
0·41 m cut off

Use the digits 3 4 6 7 0. How many additions adding to a whole number of units can you make, for example $3.4 + 0.6$ or $0.34 + 0.66$? Each digit can be used more than once.

Adding and subtracting

Choose your own method to find the missing number.

1   $7.1 + \boxed{} = 9.3$

2   $\boxed{} + 0.6 = 5.4$

3   $\boxed{} + 1.7 = 3.2$

4   $8.2 - \boxed{} = 3.8$

5   $6.7 + \boxed{} = 9.8$

6   $9.4 - \boxed{} = 4.6$

7   $5.2 + \boxed{} = 8.7$

8   $6.2 - 3.8 = \boxed{}$

9   $\boxed{} + 2.7 = 3.9$

10 $\boxed{} + 0.4 = 1.2$

11 $3.6 - \boxed{} = 0.7$

12 $8.6 - \boxed{} = 4.9$

13 $1.3 + \boxed{} = 7.4$

14 $6.9 - \boxed{} = 6.5$

15 $4.7 + \boxed{} = 8.6$

What is the difference between the two distances?

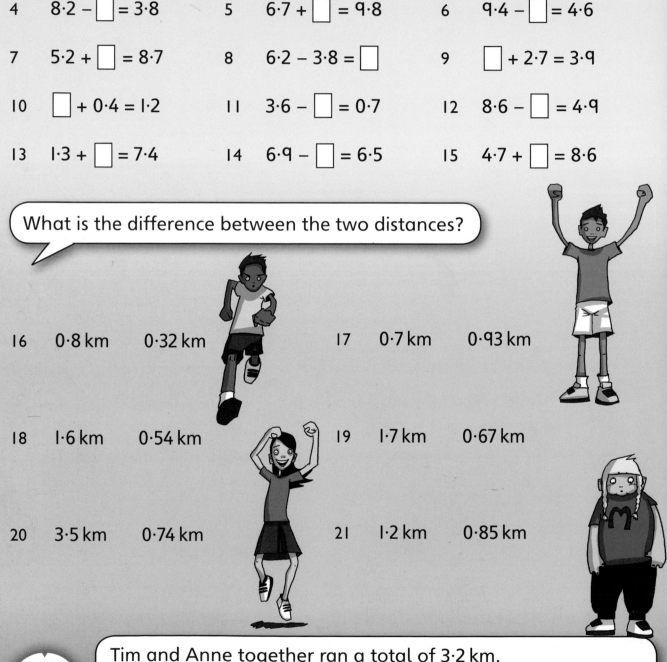

16   0·8 km   0·32 km

17   0·7 km   0·93 km

18   1·6 km   0·54 km

19   1·7 km   0·67 km

20   3·5 km   0·74 km

21   1·2 km   0·85 km

Tim and Anne together ran a total of 3·2 km.
The difference between their runs is 0·48 km. What distances could they each have run?

Adding and subtracting

Choose a method to complete these additions and subtractions.

1	0·7 − 0·21	2	0·9 − 0·48	3	0·6 − 0·43
4	0·8 − 0·17	5	6·42 − 3·31	6	4·8 − 1·35
7	4·3 + 2·81	8	3·72 + 1·46	9	7·52 − 4·81
10	5·9 − 3·27	11	0·8 − 0·63	12	1·2 + 0·71
13	3·62 − 1·51	14	3·9 + 4·71	15	1·68 + 3·42

Can you solve this subtraction: 0·31 − 0·09 = ☐? Try 0·45 − 0·09. Subtract 0·09 from other numbers. Can you find any patterns?

16 Mary-Jane has grown 0·04 m since she was last measured. She now measures 1·4 m. What did she measure previously?

17 Simon has bought 4 kg of rice but when he gets it home and weighs it, he finds he has only got 3·83 kg. How much is he missing?

18 A chemist combines 0·46 l of one chemical with 0·8 l of another. How much liquid does she then have? If 0·3 l spills, how much is left?

Adding

Add the number of pages in each book to find the total.

```
 1. 7 0 0
    3 6 4
 +  3 5 8
    7 2 2
    1 1
```

1 364 pages
  358 pages

2 428 pages
  358 pages

3 236 pages
  347 pages

4 441 pages
  275 pages

5 384 pages
  417 pages

6 326 pages
  383 pages

7 Tony had worked 328 days in 2005 and 287 days in 2004. How many days had he worked in all?

8 At a concert there were 546 women and 484 men. How many people in all attended? If 128 people came after the interval, how many were there then?

9 Sarita cycled 176 miles on her first cycling holiday and 158 miles on her second cycling holiday. How many miles did she cycle in total?

Create your own word problem for friend to answer.

```
10. 1 2 0 0
      5 6 2
 +    5 8 8
    1 1 5 0
      1 1
```

Copy and complete.

10 562 + 588

11 637 + 484

12 359 + 642

13 475 + 392

14 584 + 312

15 627 + 439

16 579 + 542

17 658 + 463

Adding

Find the total number of people at each match.

```
1.  ⑨ 0 0 0
      3 4 2 6
    + 5 8 7 8
      9 3 0 4
        1 1 1
```

1 3426 children
   5878 children

2 3578 children
   8675 adults

3 4372 children
   5683 adults

4 6955 children
   1218 adults

5 5289 children
   3476 adults

6 3143 children
   6354 adults

7 6836 children
   4734 adults

8 7668 children
   8985 adults

Explore

Arrange the cards 1–8 to make an addition of two 4-digit numbers.
What is the largest odd total you can make? What is the smallest?
What is the largest even total you can make? What is the smallest?

Copy and complete.

9   4783 + 5878 =

10 6786 + 8595 =

11 3642 + 6272 =

12 8872 + 3569 =

13 7535 + 8169 =

14 1368 + 9453 =

15 6768 + 5387 =

16 4934 + 4945 =

17 3654 + 7268 =

Adding

Complete these additions.

```
1.  10000
     4683
      742
     3604
  +    28
     9057
      211
```

```
1     4683
       742
      3604
  +     28
```

```
2     3568
        47
  +    362
```

3   1462 + 556 + 98 + 1134

4   2673 + 843 + 62 + 359

5   6437 + 362 + 12 + 1794

6   38 + 691 + 3742 + 6438

7

Choose four trips. Add the prices to find the total cost. Repeat 10 times.

Fly to Paris
£87

Weekend in
Monte Carlo
£368

Las Vegas
£2565

Sun & Surf
Down Under
£5677

Wildlife Galore
in South Africa
£1858

Icelandic cruise
£4667

Tour
America
£8874

5-day break in
Amsterdam
£475

You have £5000. Which of these trips could you choose?

Adding

Find the total miles flown.

	From	To			
1	Birmingham	Cape Town 5436	Perth 9257	Vienna 947	Paris 368
2	Washington	Berlin 4169	Chicago 597	Tokyo 6772	Rome 4434
3	Dubai	Honolulu 8530	Hong Kong 5540	Dallas 3790	London 7230
4	Cairo	Stockholm 2111	Montreal 5414	Istanbul 768	New York 5602
5	Moscow	Mexico City 6663	Paris 1544	Lisbon 1555	Warsaw 715

Explore

Look at this addition.

3684 + 5438

Find the digital root of each number.

Find the digital root of the total.

Compare your answers. What do you notice?

Try this on your own addition.

Repeat for adding three numbers, four numbers, 5-digit numbers and subtractions.

Square numbers

Write the number of pegs in each square pegboard.

1. $4 \times 4 = 16$

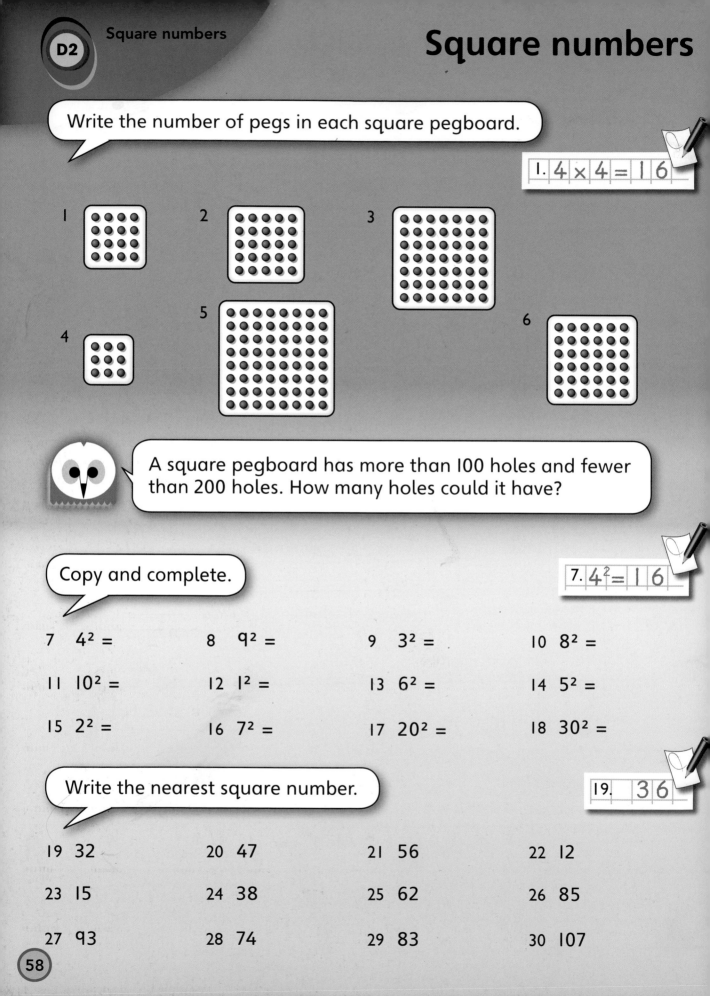

1
2
3
4
5
6

A square pegboard has more than 100 holes and fewer than 200 holes. How many holes could it have?

Copy and complete.

7. $4^2 = 16$

7 $4^2 =$

8 $9^2 =$

9 $3^2 =$

10 $8^2 =$

11 $10^2 =$

12 $1^2 =$

13 $6^2 =$

14 $5^2 =$

15 $2^2 =$

16 $7^2 =$

17 $20^2 =$

18 $30^2 =$

Write the nearest square number.

19. 36

19 32

20 47

21 56

22 12

23 15

24 38

25 62

26 85

27 93

28 74

29 83

30 107

Square numbers

Copy and complete.

1. $7^2 = 4\;9$

1. $\square^2 = 49$

2. $\square^2 = 4$

3. $\square^2 = 100$

4. $\square^2 = 9$

5. $\square^2 = 64$

6. $\square^2 = 1$

7. $\square^2 = 81$

8. $\square^2 = 25$

9. $\square^2 = 36$

Are there any square numbers whose last digit is 2? What about other digits?

Copy and complete each table.

10

Number	Square
10	100
20	400
30	
40	1600
50	2500
60	
70	
80	6400
90	
100	10 000

11

Number	Square
100	10 000
200	
300	90 000
400	
500	
600	360 000
700	490 000
800	
900	810 000
1000	

Write an estimate for these squares.

12. between 400 and 900, therefore 650

12. 25^2

13. 18^2

14. 84^2

15. 750^2

16. 650^2

17. 320^2

18. 94^2

19. 145^2

Square numbers

Write the length of the sides of these square stamps.

1. 3 0 mm

1 Area = 900 mm²

2 Area = 3600 mm²

3 Area = 400 mm²

4 Area = 2500 mm²

5 Area = 6400 mm²

6 Area = 1600 mm²

If the post office has sheets of 10 by 10 of each stamp, investigate the size of each sheet in centimetres.

7

Copy and complete this table.

10^2	20^2	30^2	40^2	50^2	60^2	70^2	80^2	90^2	100^2
100				2500			6400		

Use the table to help you write an estimate for each square number.

8. 2 0 0

8 14^2

9 33^2

10 91^2

11 23^2

12 49^2

13 78^2

14 18^2

15 97^2

Use a calculator to find the exact square number.

Explore

Investigate the squares of these numbers: 15^2, 25^2, 35^2, 45^2.
Can you spot a pattern?
Can you use this pattern to help you say, mentally, the square of any of these numbers?

Square numbers

Use a calculator and trial and error to help you complete these:

7. $8^2 = 64$

1 $\boxed{}^2 = 64$ 2 $\boxed{}^2 = 196$ 3 $\boxed{}^2 = 625$

4 $\boxed{}^2 = 289$ 5 $\boxed{}^2 = 441$ 6 $\boxed{}^2 = 1024$

7 $\boxed{}^2 = 361$ 8 $\boxed{}^2 = 1681$ 9 $\boxed{}^2 = 2809$

Who am I?

10 We are two square numbers. When we are added together, the result is another square number.

11 I am a 2-digit multiple of 10, more than 30. When I am squared, the total of my digits is another square number.

12 We are two square numbers. The difference between us is another square number.

13 I am a 3-digit multiple of 100. My square is a quarter of a million.

14 I am a 2-digit multiple of 10. When I am squared I am between 4000 and 5000.

15 I am a 2-digit multiple of 5. When I am squared my hundreds digit is 6.

Explore

32 is happy because:

32 — Square each digit then add

9 + 4 = 13

1 + 9 = 10

1 + 0 = 1

Repeat until you arrive at a 1-digit number

If you arrive at 1, then the start number is happy.
Investigate how many happy numbers you can find up to 100.

Write the next four numbers in each sequence:

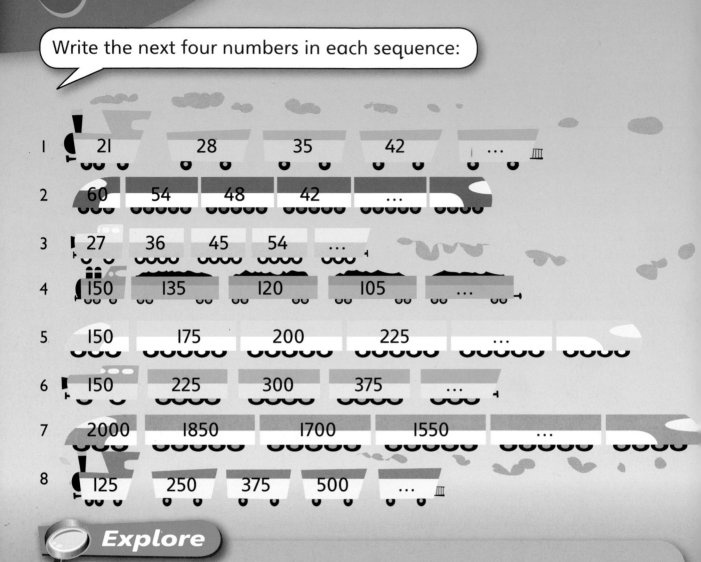

1 21   28   35   42   …

2 60 54 48 42 …

3 27 36 45 54 …

4 150 135 120 105 …

5 150 175 200 225 …

6 150 225 300 375 …

7 2000 1850 1700 1550 …

8 125 250 375 500 …

Explore

This sequence is called the Fibonacci sequence.

1, 1, 2, 3, 5, 8, 13…

Can you spot the rule for creating the sequence?

Find the tenth numbers in sequences that start with these two numbers, using the same rule:

9   2, 1   10   3, 2   11   1, 5

12   4, 1   13 $^-$1, 1   14   7, 8

Decimal and fraction sequences

Write the next four numbers in each sequence:

1 | 2 | 2·5 | 3 | 3·5 | ...

2 | 0·4 | 0·5 | 0·6 | 0·7 | ...

3 | 1·1 | 1·3 | 1·5 | 1·7 | ...

4 | 1·5 | 1·75 | 2 | 2·25 | ...

5 | 0·2 | 0·6 | 1 | 1·4 | ...

6 | 3 | 4·5 | 6 | 7·5 | ...

7 | 4 | 4·2 | 4·4 | 4·6 | ...

8 | 10 | 12·5 | 15 | 17·5 | ...

9 | 5 | 5·75 | 6·5 | 7·25 | ...

10 | 0·8 | 3·1 | 5·4 | 7·7 | ...

Write the missing numbers in these sequences:

11 $2\frac{1}{3}$, $2\frac{2}{3}$, 3, ____, $3\frac{2}{3}$, ____

12 $2\frac{1}{4}$, $2\frac{3}{4}$, $3\frac{1}{4}$, ____, ____, $4\frac{3}{4}$

13 $3\frac{1}{3}$, $3\frac{2}{3}$, 4, ____, $4\frac{2}{3}$, ____

14 $1\frac{1}{2}$, ____, 3, ____, $4\frac{1}{2}$, ____, 6

Invent some decimal and fraction sequences of your own, each with one missing number. Invite a friend to find the missing numbers.

Triangular numbers

Write the number of cubes in each set.

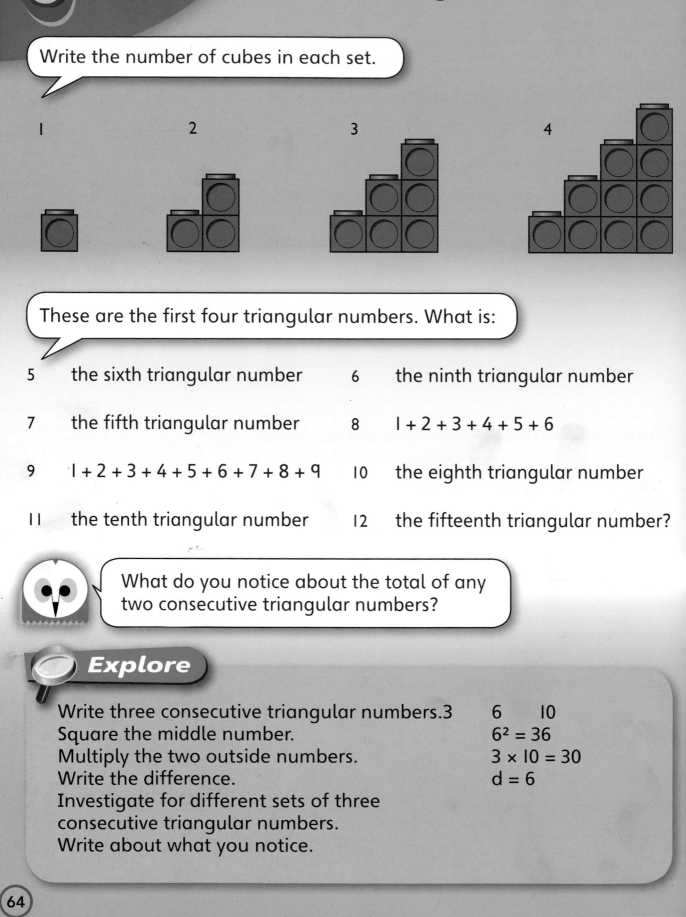

1   2   3   4

These are the first four triangular numbers. What is:

5   the sixth triangular number   6   the ninth triangular number

7   the fifth triangular number   8   1 + 2 + 3 + 4 + 5 + 6

9   1 + 2 + 3 + 4 + 5 + 6 + 7 + 8 + 9   10   the eighth triangular number

11   the tenth triangular number   12   the fifteenth triangular number?

What do you notice about the total of any two consecutive triangular numbers?

Explore

Write three consecutive triangular numbers.3   6   10
Square the middle number.   6² = 36
Multiply the two outside numbers.   3 × 10 = 30
Write the difference.   d = 6
Investigate for different sets of three
consecutive triangular numbers.
Write about what you notice.

Multiplying

Copy and complete these multiplications.

1 (1500)
   528
  ×   3
    24
    60
  1500
  ———

2 (2000)
   464
  ×   4
    16
   240
  ———

3 (4200)
   732
  ×   6
    12
  ———

Now try these.

4   326
  × 4

5   458
  × 3

6   724
  × 6

7   562
  × 4

8   395
  × 5

9   643
  × 4

10   527
  × 7

11   741
  × 3

Doughnuts are sold in boxes of four. Calculate how many doughnuts were sold each week.

12 Week 1
426 boxes

13 Week 2
148 boxes

14 Week 3
276 boxes

15 Week 4
325 boxes

16 Week 5
542 boxes

17 Week 6
441 boxes

If a doughnut costs 5p to make, and a box of four doughnuts is sold for 45p, investigate how much profit the company makes each week.

Multiplying

Copy and complete these multiplications.

1 (24000)
```
  4312
×    6
─────
    12
    60
  1800
 24000
─────
```

2 (   )
```
  5473
×    4
─────
    12
   280
─────
```

3 (   )
```
  3627
×    5
─────
    35
─────
```

4 (   )
```
  4263
×    4
─────
─────
```

Now try these.

5   3725
    ×   4
    ─────

6   4368
    ×   3
    ─────

7   5274
    ×   6
    ─────

8   3429
    ×   4
    ─────

9   1438
    ×   7
    ─────

10 2546
    ×   8
    ─────

11 3472
    ×   5
    ─────

12 4135
    ×   6
    ─────

Cupcakes are sold in boxes of six. How many cupcakes were sold each month?

13 January
    1382 boxes

14 February
    2047 boxes

15 March
    1943 boxes

16 April
    2264 boxes

17 May
    1783 boxes

18 June
    1452 boxes

19 July
    1874 boxes

20 August
    2139 boxes

21 September
    1276 boxes

If 2526 boxes are sold each month, approximately how many months will it take to sell a million boxes?

Multiplying

These children used number cards to create a multiplication. They tried to get an answer close to 10 000. Predict the two nearest answers, then complete each child's multiplication to find out who was the nearest, next nearest, and so on…

1.
	9	0	0	0
	4	5	3	7
	×			2

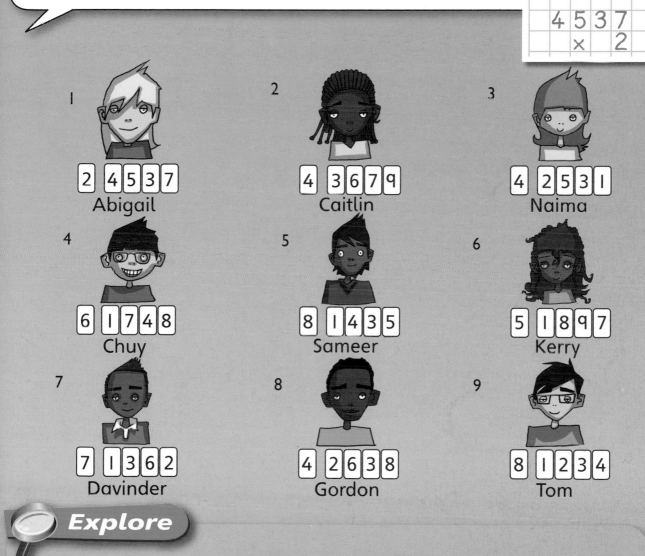

1 [2] [4][5][3][7]
Abigail

2 [4] [3][6][7][9]
Caitlin

3 [4] [2][5][3][1]
Naima

4 [6] [1][7][4][8]
Chuy

5 [8] [1][4][3][5]
Sameer

6 [5] [1][8][9][7]
Kerry

7 [7] [1][3][6][2]
Davinder

8 [4] [2][6][3][8]
Gordon

9 [8] [1][2][3][4]
Tom

Explore

Use number cards 1–9.

Create a 4-digit number and a 1-digit number, and multiply them together.   [5] [1][7][4][6]

Investigate how many multiplications you can create with an answer between 8000 and 9000.

Arrange the digits to create these multiplications.

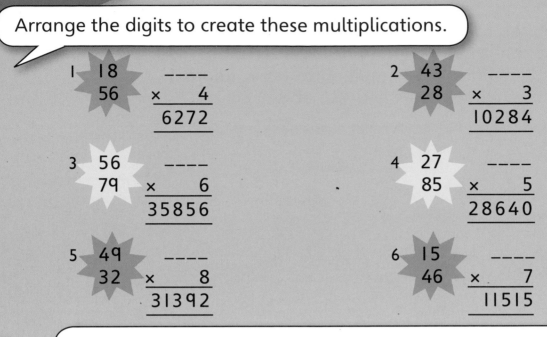

1.
```
  18    ----
  56  ×    4
      6272
```

2.
```
  43    ----
  28  ×    3
     10284
```

3.
```
  56    ----
  79  ×    6
     35856
```

4.
```
  27    ----
  85  ×    5
     28640
```

5.
```
  49    ----
  32  ×    8
     31392
```

6.
```
  15    ----
  46  ×    7
     11515
```

Can you create a multiplication like this: ☐ × ☐☐☐☐, so that the digits in the answer are in ascending order or descending order, e.g. 1369 or 9421? The multiplier cannot be 1!

7 4732 people attended the theatre last week, each paying £8 for a ticket. The theatre company were hoping to receive takings of £40 000. How much more or less did they take?

8 The 'Smoothcrews' ship sails around the Caribbean. It needs a full overhaul after sailing 30 000 miles. It sails a total of 2768 miles every year for 6 years. How many more miles can it sail before needing an overhaul?

9 A 'Round the World' holiday costs £4286. Children travel half-price What is the cost for a family of four adults and three children?

10 8692 people attended Rovers' last match. They all gave 5p to a charity. How much was collected? How much more would have been collected if they had given 8p instead?

Fractions of amounts

For each pair of coloured grids, write the coloured fractions.

1. $\frac{1}{4}$ of $8 = 2$

$\frac{3}{4}$ of $8 = 6$

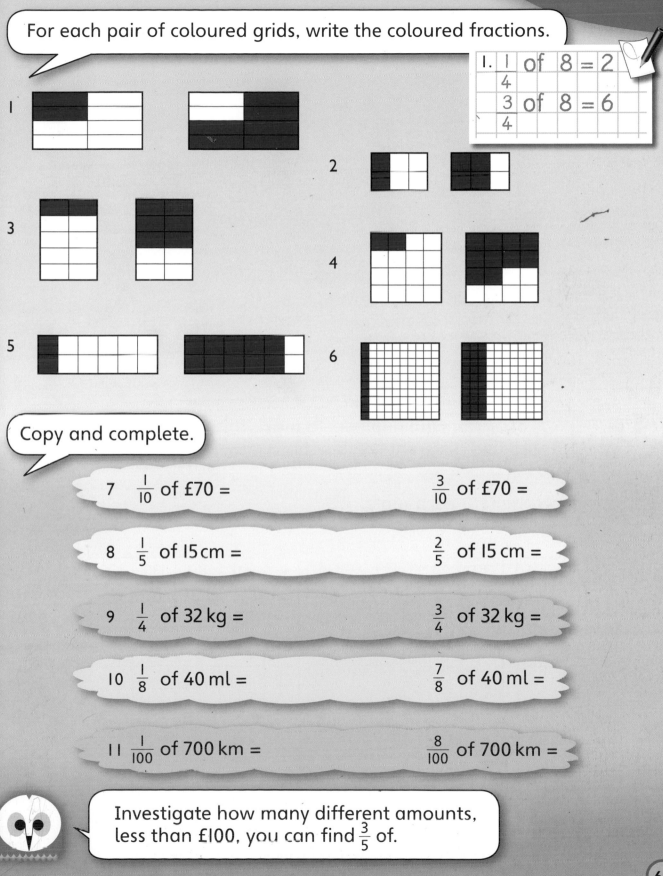

1

2

3

4

5

6

Copy and complete.

7   $\frac{1}{10}$ of £70 = $\frac{3}{10}$ of £70 =

8   $\frac{1}{5}$ of 15 cm = $\frac{2}{5}$ of 15 cm =

9   $\frac{1}{4}$ of 32 kg = $\frac{3}{4}$ of 32 kg =

10   $\frac{1}{8}$ of 40 ml = $\frac{7}{8}$ of 40 ml =

11   $\frac{1}{100}$ of 700 km = $\frac{8}{100}$ of 700 km =

Investigate how many different amounts, less than £100, you can find $\frac{3}{5}$ of.

Fractions of amounts

Write the weight of each fraction.

1 400 g

a $\dfrac{7}{100}$ b $\dfrac{18}{100}$ c $\dfrac{51}{100}$ d $\dfrac{3}{10}$ e $\dfrac{7}{10}$ f $\dfrac{9}{10}$

2 600 g

a $\dfrac{9}{100}$ b $\dfrac{11}{100}$ c $\dfrac{21}{100}$ d $\dfrac{4}{10}$ e $\dfrac{9}{10}$ f $\dfrac{6}{10}$

3 1 kg

a $\dfrac{3}{100}$ b $\dfrac{28}{100}$ c $\dfrac{47}{100}$ d $\dfrac{7}{10}$ e $\dfrac{3}{10}$ f $\dfrac{8}{10}$

$\dfrac{\square}{\square}$ of $\square = 15$. Find numbers to make this work.
Try to find different combinations.

Copy and complete each table.

4

×	20	60	30	70
$\dfrac{1}{2}$				
$\dfrac{3}{5}$				
$\dfrac{3}{10}$				

5

×	40	80	130	420
$\dfrac{7}{10}$				
$\dfrac{2}{5}$				
$\dfrac{1}{4}$				

6

×	200	600	500	900
$\dfrac{1}{100}$				
$\dfrac{4}{5}$				
$\dfrac{21}{100}$				

7

×	300	700	1400	400
$\dfrac{33}{100}$				
$\dfrac{9}{10}$				
$\dfrac{83}{100}$				

Fractions of amounts

Find the fraction of each amount.

1 £48   a $\frac{2}{3}$ b $\frac{3}{4}$ c $\frac{5}{6}$ d $\frac{7}{12}$ e $\frac{5}{8}$ f $\frac{1}{24}$

2 £40   a $\frac{3}{4}$ b $\frac{4}{5}$ c $\frac{7}{8}$ d $\frac{11}{20}$ e $\frac{9}{10}$ f $\frac{3}{20}$

3 £120   a $\frac{2}{3}$ b $\frac{7}{12}$ c $\frac{8}{15}$ d $\frac{5}{6}$ e $\frac{3}{5}$ f $\frac{17}{20}$

If $\frac{3}{4}$ of A is the same as $\frac{2}{3}$ of B, what could A and B be?

Copy and complete.

4 $\frac{2}{3}$ of £6 =

5 $\frac{3}{4}$ of £48 =

6 $\frac{4}{5}$ of £30 =

7 $\frac{5}{6}$ of £24 =

8 $\frac{7}{12}$ of £24 =

9 $\frac{9}{10}$ of £120 =

10 $\frac{3}{8}$ of £48 =

11 $\frac{4}{7}$ of £28 =

12 $\frac{5}{9}$ of £72 =

13 $\frac{4}{11}$ of £88 =

14 $\frac{7}{20}$ of £120 =

15 $\frac{11}{25}$ of £250 =

Explore

Use cards 0–9.
Use the cards to make a fraction of an amount. $\frac{3}{5}$ of $\boxed{6}\boxed{0}$

Write it with the answer. $\frac{3}{5}$ of 60 = 36

Investigate how many you can make with a denominator of 5.
Investigate for other denominators.

Fractions of amounts

In each list, write a guess for the smallest and largest. Calculate each amount to see if your guess was correct.

> 1. Guess: largest   b
>   smallest d
>   a) $\frac{1}{3}$ of 60 = 20, $\frac{2}{3}$ of 60 = 40

1 a $\frac{2}{3}$ of 60   b $\frac{3}{4}$ of 80   c $\frac{4}{5}$ of 50   d $\frac{5}{7}$ of 70

2 a $\frac{3}{5}$ of 25   b $\frac{5}{6}$ of 18   c $\frac{3}{4}$ of 16   d $\frac{3}{5}$ of 20

3 a $\frac{4}{9}$ of 36   b $\frac{3}{7}$ of 49   c $\frac{4}{5}$ of 35   d $\frac{2}{3}$ of 27

4 a $\frac{7}{10}$ of 90   b $\frac{11}{100}$ of 700   c $\frac{9}{50}$ of 400   d $\frac{3}{25}$ of 250

5 a $\frac{5}{12}$ of 60   b $\frac{7}{11}$ of 77   c $\frac{8}{15}$ of 90   d $\frac{9}{20}$ of 80

Write a list like these for your friend to order. The answers should be between 50 and 60.

6 200 pupils voted for their favourite lesson. $\frac{2}{5}$ voted for maths, $\frac{3}{10}$ voted for art, $\frac{1}{4}$ voted for science, and the remainder couldn't make up their minds! How many pupils are undecided?

7  Graham collects football stickers. There are 120 in a set. Last week he had collected $\frac{3}{5}$ of them, but now he has $\frac{3}{4}$. How many stickers has he collected this week?

8 Ruby has saved £4·80, but she owes $\frac{3}{8}$ of this to her brother and $\frac{1}{12}$ to her sister. How much will she have left when she pays them what she owes?

Fractions and decimals

Write each coloured part as a fraction, then write it as a number of hundredths.

$$1. \quad \frac{1}{4} = \frac{25}{100}$$

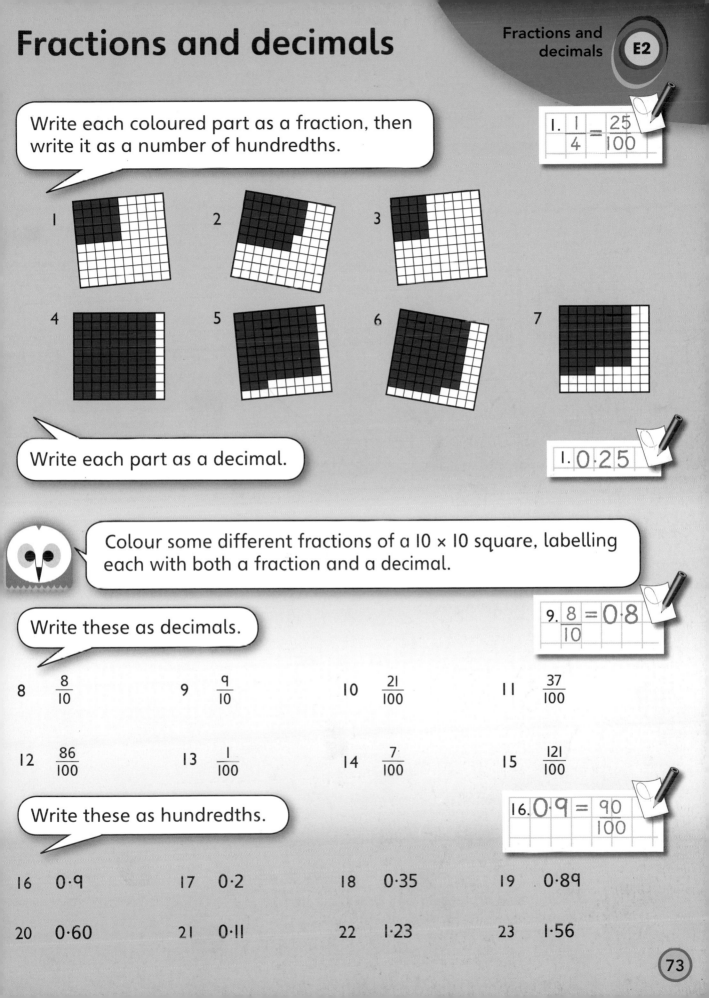

1   2   3

4   5   6   7

Write each part as a decimal.

1. 0.25

Colour some different fractions of a 10 × 10 square, labelling each with both a fraction and a decimal.

$$9. \quad \frac{8}{10} = 0.8$$

Write these as decimals.

8 $\frac{8}{10}$

9 $\frac{9}{10}$

10 $\frac{21}{100}$

11 $\frac{37}{100}$

12 $\frac{86}{100}$

13 $\frac{1}{100}$

14 $\frac{7}{100}$

15 $\frac{121}{100}$

$$16. \quad 0.9 = \frac{90}{100}$$

Write these as hundredths.

16   0·9

17   0·2

18   0·35

19   0·89

20   0·60

21   0·11

22   1·23

23   1·56

Fractions and decimals

Write the position of each pointer as a fraction and as a decimal.

$1.a) \dfrac{7}{10} = 0.7$

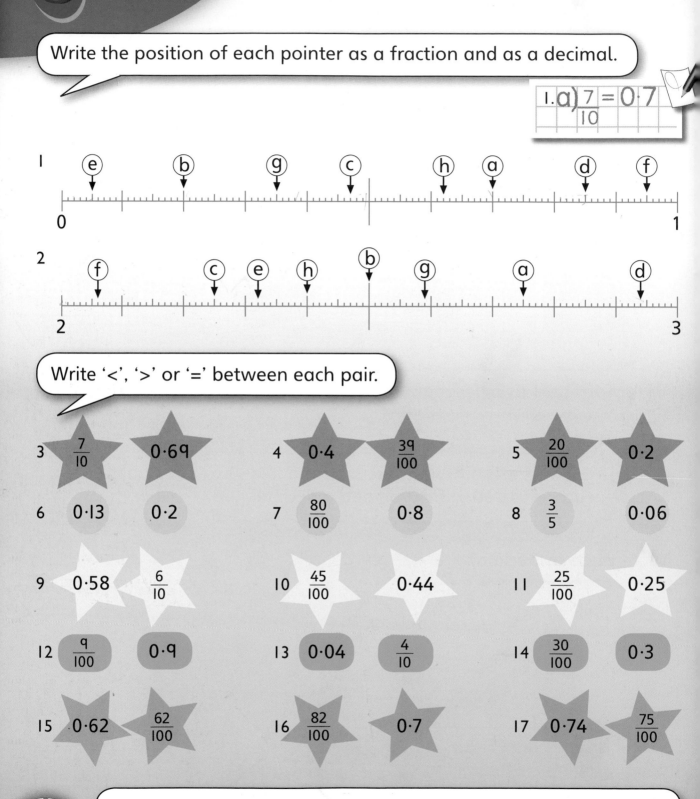

Write '<', '>' or '=' between each pair.

3 $\dfrac{7}{10}$ ⭐ 0.69 ⭐ 4 0.4 ⭐ $\dfrac{39}{100}$ ⭐ 5 $\dfrac{20}{100}$ ⭐ 0.2 ⭐

6 0.13 0.2 7 $\dfrac{80}{100}$ 0.8 8 $\dfrac{3}{5}$ 0.06

9 0.58 $\dfrac{6}{10}$ 10 $\dfrac{45}{100}$ 0.44 11 $\dfrac{25}{100}$ 0.25

12 $\dfrac{9}{100}$ 0.9 13 0.04 $\dfrac{4}{10}$ 14 $\dfrac{30}{100}$ 0.3

15 0.62 $\dfrac{62}{100}$ 16 $\dfrac{82}{100}$ 0.7 17 0.74 $\dfrac{75}{100}$

Invent five more pairs, each using an equals sign between them. Write three numbers (a mixture of fractions and decimals) to make □ < □ < □ or □ > □ > □

Fractions and decimals

1.045

Write as a decimal.

1 $\frac{1}{10}$ more than 0·35

2 $\frac{1}{10}$ less than 0·72

3 $\frac{1}{100}$ more than 0·46

4 $\frac{1}{100}$ less than 0·3

5 $\frac{14}{100}$ more than 1·9

6 $\frac{21}{100}$ less than 0·75

7 $\frac{175}{1000}$ more than 0·423

8 $\frac{155}{1000}$ less than 0·6

Explore

Use cards 0–9, and a counter for a decimal point.
Create a fraction and its equivalent decimal.

$\frac{4}{5}$ = 0 · 8

$\frac{3}{4}$ = 0 · 7 5

Investigate how many sets you can make.

Write each set in order, smallest to largest. You can use a calculator.

9 $\frac{3}{5}$ $\frac{1}{4}$ $\frac{21}{100}$ 0·4 0·27

10 $\frac{7}{10}$ $\frac{3}{4}$ $\frac{78}{100}$ 0·72 0·8

11 $\frac{4}{5}$ $\frac{85}{100}$ $\frac{9}{10}$ 0·815 0·82

12 0·85 0·855 $\frac{7}{8}$ $\frac{13}{16}$ $\frac{86}{100}$

13 0·55 0·535 0·5 $\frac{9}{16}$ $\frac{13}{25}$

14 $1\frac{3}{4}$ $\frac{15}{8}$ 1·725 1·7 1·82

15 $2\frac{1}{2}$ $\frac{9}{4}$ 2·35 2·3 2·535

16 4·275 4·24 4·3 $4\frac{1}{5}$ $4\frac{3}{8}$

Fractions and decimals

Write these fractions as decimals.
You can use a calculator to help you.

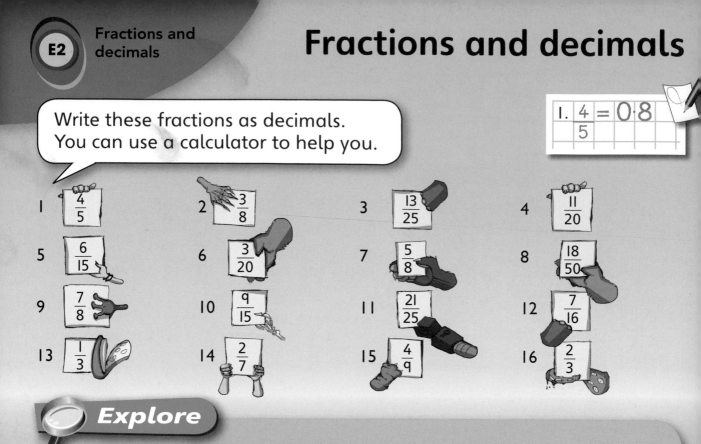

1. $\frac{4}{5} = 0.8$

1 $\frac{4}{5}$ 2 $\frac{3}{8}$ 3 $\frac{13}{25}$ 4 $\frac{11}{20}$

5 $\frac{6}{15}$ 6 $\frac{3}{20}$ 7 $\frac{5}{8}$ 8 $\frac{18}{50}$

9 $\frac{7}{8}$ 10 $\frac{9}{15}$ 11 $\frac{21}{25}$ 12 $\frac{7}{16}$

13 $\frac{1}{3}$ 14 $\frac{2}{7}$ 15 $\frac{4}{9}$ 16 $\frac{2}{3}$

Explore

Use cards 2–9, and a calculator.

Choose two of the cards and arrange them to create a fraction.

Write the fraction as a decimal.   = 0·375

Investigate how many fractions and their corresponding decimals you can create.

Investigate how many you can find that have three or more decimal places.

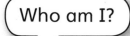
Who am I?

17 I am a proper fraction with a denominator of 20. My decimal equivalent is 0·6.

18 I am a decimal number between $1\frac{1}{2}$ and 2. My equivalent fraction has a numerator and denominator which total 11.

19 I am an improper fraction with a denominator of 5. My decimal equivalent is 4·6.

20 I am a mixed number between 1 and 2. My fraction has a denominator of 20. As a decimal my digits total 9.

Tests for divisibility

1	2	3	4	5	6	7	8	9	10
11	12	13	14	15	16	17	18	19	20
21	22	23	24	25	26	27	28	29	30
31	32	33	34	35	36	37	38	39	40
41	42	43	44	45	46	47	48	49	50
51	52	53	54	55	56	57	58	59	60
61	62	63	64	65	66	67	68	69	70
71	72	73	74	75	76	77	78	79	80
81	82	83	84	85	86	87	88	89	90
91	92	93	94	95	96	97	98	99	100

Multiples of 3

1	2	3	4	5	6	7	8	9	10
11	12	13	14	15	16	17	18	19	20
21	22	23	24	25	26	27	28	29	30
31	32	33	34	35	36	37	38	39	40
41	42	43	44	45	46	47	48	49	50
51	52	53	54	55	56	57	58	59	60
61	62	63	64	65	66	67	68	69	70
71	72	73	74	75	76	77	78	79	80
81	82	83	84	85	86	87	88	89	90
91	92	93	94	95	96	97	98	99	100

Multiples of 6

1. If a number is divisible by 3, then...

Look at the digit totals of the numbers. Write a rule for testing:

1 divisibility by 3   2 divisibility by 6   3 divisibility by 9

Can you invent a rule for testing divisibility by 18?

Are these numbers divisible by 3? Write 'Yes' or 'No'.

4. Yes

4	48	5	76	6	87	7	139
8	251	9	108	10	347	11	216
12	1429	13	3513	14	1648	15	2039

Tests for divisibility

True or false?

1. 1102 is divisible by 2

2. 346 is divisible by 6

3. 9090 is divisible by 10

4. 1089 is divisible by 9

5. 215 is divisible by 3

6. 1875 is divisible by 3 and 5

7. 342 is divisible by 6

8. 495 is divisible by 3 and 5

9. 369 is divisible by 3 and 6

10. 3240 is divisible by 6 and 5

Create one true and one false sentence for a number divisible by 6. Repeat for divisibility by other numbers.

96   78   372   124   39   56
216   192   432   175   289   1044

Write which of the numbers are divisible by:

11. 2

12. 4

13. 8

14. 3

15. 6

16. 9

17. 10

18. 25

19. 50

Are these numbers divisible by 25? Write 'Yes' or 'No'.

20. Yes

20. 325

21. 175

22. 415

23. 865

24. 9000

25. 2775

26. 4320

27. 3025

28. 2750

29. 6155

30. 7080

31. 81 350

Tests for divisibility

1 Copy and complete the table. Write a tick to show that the number is divisible by any of the headings.

	2	3	4	5	6	8	9	10	25	50
140	✓			✓						
270										
3000										
85										
76										
432										
175										
234										
875										
4134										

Can you find any numbers that will have 6 ticks, 7 ticks, 8 ticks, 9 ticks, 10 ticks?

2 I am divisible by 3 but not by 6. I am between 25 and 30.

3 I am divisible by both 2 and 3. I am less than 50 and I am a square number.

4 I am not divisible by 2, 3, 4, 5, 6, 7, 8 or 9. I am between 32 and 40.

5 I am divisible by 7, and my units digit is 6.

6 I am divisible by 8 and my digits have a total of 9.

7 I am not divisible by 2, 4, 5, 6 or 9, but I am divisible by 3. I am between 60 and 85.

Tests for divisibility

1 If a number is divisible by 3 and divisible by 4, then it must be divisible by 12.

2 If a number is divisible by 3, it must be an odd number.

3 If a number is divisible by 9, then it must be divisible by 3.

4 If a number is divisible by 6, it must be an even number.

5 If a number is divisible by 5 and by 7, then it must be an odd number.

6 There is only one number less than 100 that is divisible by both 7 and 8.

7 There are five numbers less than 100 that are divisible by both 3 and 5.

8 If a number is divisible by 9, then it cannot be divisible by 5.

Explore

Matt thinks he has discovered a test for divisibility by 7 for 3-digit numbers, for example 6 3 7.

He says: double the hundreds digit.

double 6 = 12

Then add it to the remaining part of the number.

12 + 37 = 49

If the resulting 2-digit number is divisible by 7, then so is the 3-digit number.

Investigate the method for different 3-digit numbers to test Matt's discovery.